THE Map OF THE SOUL

DISCOVERING YOUR TRUE PURPOSE

Tricia Brennan

ROCKPOOL
PUBLISHING

D1205165

A Rockpool book
Published by Rockpool Publishing
24 Constitution Road, Dulwich Hill, NSW 2203, Australia
www.rockpoolpublishing.com.au

First published in 2011
Copyright © Tricia Brennan, 2011

National Library of Australia Cataloguing-in-Publication entry
Brennan, Tricia.
The map of the soul : discovering your true purpose / Tricia Brennan.
1st ed.

9781921295331 (pbk.)

Self-actualization (Psychology)
Success--Psychological aspects.

158.1

Cover and internal design and typsetting by Seymour Design
Edited by Gabiann Marin
Printed and bound in China by Everbest Printing Co Ltd

10 9 8 7 6 5 4 3 2 1

Tricia Brennan is an internationally acclaimed intuitive counselor, author and spiritual teacher. Prior to devoting herself full-time to assisting others, Tricia had a highly successful 20-year career as an art director in the advertising and film industries.

As a gifted visionary, Tricia has guided thousands of people on journeys of self-discovery and to acknowledge their true potential. Her heightened perceptive abilities allow her to retrieve valuable information from the subconscious of an individual and decipher messages from the Higher Realms and her wisdom and insight enable her to pinpoint a person's core issues and life lessons with great ease and accuracy.

As well as facilitating internationally recognised seminars for individuals, groups and couples, based on the insights contained in *The Map of the Soul; Discovering your True Purpose*, Tricia has also published three books – *Looking Beyond the Mirror, Facing the Dawn* and *Vision and Heart*. and created a number of successful audio meditation series including – *The Art of Balance; The Stress First Aid Kit; Attracting Love*, and *Body Transformation from the Inside Out*.

For more information on Tricia's books, podcasts, CDs, seminars and retreats log on to the following website – **www.triciabrennan.com**

For more information about discovering your True Purpose please visit www.mapofthesoul.com

CONTENTS

Part One
The Map of the Soul –
Uncovering the Truth.
The Basic Principles.

Part Two
Creating New Maps –
Aligning with your Authentic Self.

3. LOGGING THE MAP OF THE SOUL 47
The Basic Tools
Soul-Speak – The Soul's Whispers
Intuition – Your Inner Compass
Life-Speak – Your World as a Mirror
Dream-Speak – Your Inner Landscape
Body-Speak – Your Physical Vehicle
Journaling
Affirmations
Contemplation
Meditation
Setting your Intention

Part Three
THE TWELVE LEVEL COURSE
The Journey of Self Discovery

Acknowledgements

I am sincerely grateful to the beautiful King family who offered their loving support during my writing process. To Aldo for his generosity, to Luca for being such a wonderful source of joy in my world and a special thanks to Tania for her unwavering encouragement and invaluable help developing the manuscript.

I would also like to extend my heartfelt gratitude to Fleur Brown, Ken Outch, Selwa Anthony and Lisa Hanrahan for their generous contribution in helping me take this book out into the world and for believing in my work.

Finally, I would like to offer a special note of thanks to my seen and unseen friends, especially Lazaris, for teaching me about the true meaning of love and helping me to uncover more of the truth.

Introduction

My Story & How This Book Came About

As an intuitive counselor, my capacity to 'read' people is based on my clairaudient, clairsentient and clairvoyant abilities. My perceptive nature allows me to go beyond the identity of an individual and uncover their deepest fears, aspirations and fundamental beliefs. Working with people in this way has helped me realize that no matter who we are, where we live, or what we do; we all seek a deeper experience of love and greater freedom.

Over the course of 20 years I have spent a lot of my time helping many wealthy, powerful and attractive people unravel the mystery of why, despite their vast achievements, they are still not completely happy. I have counseled corporate executives, housewives, Hollywood celebrities, professors, doctors, therapists and even renowned spiritual teachers. No matter what their identity, they all asked similar questions:

Does our life have a higher purpose or is it merely a series of random events?

Do unseen forces influence the course of our fate?

Can we trust our intuition?

Do we each have a Soul mate?

What is my Soul's Purpose?

These are some of the questions I address in this book, based on almost half a decade of gathering wisdom. My search for truth has taken me from my childhood home in Sydney to temples in India and on to the New Mexico desert. That quest has brought me face-to-face with both enlightened beings and charlatans – each presenting a valuable lesson on unity and oneness and the importance of following our intuition. Eventually that philosophy became my personal truth as my external search came to an end and I realized the validity of my Soul.

This realization is, for each of us, the most important journey we can ever make – discovering the phenomenal gifts that rest at the heart of our essence. Therefore, rather than present you with all of the answers, I will guide you through the process to glean those insights for yourself. By teaching you how to create a deeper relationship with your inner-self, I trust you will eventually be led by your Soul's whispers in the same way I was.

'When we enter the physical world we develop amnesia, losing sight of our true origin and the greater parts of ourselves. Life's little mysteries are only revealed if we are willing to lift the veil of forgetfulness.'

Scanning the covers of the glossy magazines that rest on our newsstands, it is easy to see that we live in a world where 'performance and appearance' are celebrated more often than a person's essence and the quality of their heart. Sadly, the labels we attach to ourselves have come to warrant what we expect from life and often establish our sense of worth. Whether we are a student, a mother or the CEO of a large company, we start the day with a long 'to do list', becoming a slave to time.

Keeping up with the demands and the pace of the modern world, we can easily fall prey to the silent chant, 'keep up or get left behind'. But how often do we stop in our tracks and ask ourselves where we are ultimately heading, or even pause to consider the purpose of our life? We fall asleep under the ego's spell and become far too attached to our identity – believing that it alone will get us what we want. Yet we are challenged when it comes to connecting with our Soul, or our deeper essence – which is where the source of true happiness lies.

Unfortunately it often takes a crisis to interrupt the habitual flow of our lives and force us to do a little 'Soul searching' and look more closely at the framework of our lives. For me that awakening came very early in life during a near death experience.

When I was four years old I drowned and was drawn upward, towards a shimmering light. I heard a whirring sound and my inner senses came to life. My awareness became sharp and clear as I detached from the boundaries of my physical body.

My Spirit soared and all of a sudden I had a bird's eye view of an undulating ocean dappled with dancing lights. The lenses I normally saw life through had altered to give me a greater perspective. I hovered above the beach and saw my mother talking to her friend, oblivious to my predicament. As I focused on certain people on the beach, I could hear their thoughts and somehow knew what they were feeling. My hearing was acute, yet I knew I was listening through my inner ears. It was like being an observer in a dream, except the colors seemed more vivid.

I was reluctant to leave this blissful state in which I felt so light and free. Then I heard a soft voice whisper, 'Go back, dear one, it's not your time.' The words echoed in my mind, coaxing me back into my body, until the whispers faded and my brother rescued me.

Based on human logic I should have been dead. On that miraculous day, time had stood still just long enough to open a window into a whole new dimension I had seen firsthand that there was so much more to life than what we see with our physical eyes and I was not going to forget it. When I returned to my body I left a portal open to an incredible realm, which I have spent much of my lifetime investigating.

In following that quest, I eventually realized that when we first enter the physical world we develop amnesia, losing sight of our true origin and the greater parts of ourselves.

My next awakening came one Sunday afternoon at the age of eleven when I was overwhelmed with a desire to write. Within 10 minutes I wrote a page of information that offered my sister wise counsel on how to alter the course of her life. The information sent shivers through her body and she was overwhelmed with emotion. Not clear where the message had come from, my investigation revealed a quiet voice that emerged from deep beneath my logical thoughts – ultimately known as my Soul's whispers. From that day on, the messages I received were always comforting, encouraging and wise; and eventually became the basis of my work as a spiritual teacher.

Each and every one of us has the potential to become enlightened by embracing our own Soul's whispers and discovering our true potential. The first step is 'being still' and listening to our intuition.

When people first meet me in a session, they are surprised I know so much about them. Yet it is not that surprising, I simply listen for sounds, see images and register feelings that normally go unnoticed. Although everyone has the latent capacity to do this, I have honed the skill over the course of my life until it has become second nature. The answer as to how I obtain the information is simple.

On a Soul level, we are intrinsically connected by an invisible thread: we are all one. By entering the heart of stillness, I learnt to hear the 'unspoken word' communicated beneath our rambling thoughts. It is within that sacred silence that we commune with our Soul and connect with the essence of life itself.

Although I have been meditating since I was a child, my intuitive senses didn't develop overnight. Like all of us, I was born with a spark of promise; but I nourished it with my desire to know more about our human potential. Rather than solely look for answers in the outside world, eventually I turned my focus within to create a deeper, more rewarding connection with my Soul.

For each of us, that is ultimately the most rewarding path we can ever follow – a personal quest that leads to love, joy, individuality and freedom. There is nothing missing within any of us: we are all whole and complete. That is why I have chosen to guide you toward deepening the relationship you have with your Authentic Self.

You are so much more than your body, your mind, or even your Spirit; you are an integral part of All That Is. All you need to do to claim this greatest truth is to adjust the lenses you see life through until you finally see 'the bigger picture'.

An Overview of this Book

**'The Key to Love Rests in your Heart and the
Formula for Success Lies in your Mind.'**

You have potentially picked up this book because you may feel as though there is something missing in your life, or you are seeking a deeper sense of meaning and purpose. Some of the information you receive may challenge your current perceptions or beliefs about life and the nature of your relationships. However the principles put forward have been used from the beginning of creation as we know it, and govern our human experience according to laws of metaphysics.

This book will help you explore the Map of your Soul and uncover more of your True Self. It will allow you to get in touch with your genuine preferences and align with True North – the path of graceful creation. The information I offer is based on my observations working with clients over 20 years – people from all walks of life who were searching for hope in a world where 'proving our worth' has become automatic. No matter who they were, or how many of the trappings of success they had accrued in life, in some area they still believed they weren't good enough.

To awaken more of my client's true potential, I merely shone a torch on the sleeping parts of their Soul that were waiting to be acknowledged. By reading through the information presented in this book, you will be given the opportunity to do precisely the same.

I will guide you every step of the way until you are able to lead yourself in collaboration with your Higher Self and Soul. I am merely an intermediary helping you build a stronger connection with these guides.

The way you earnestly begin the process is by 'looking beyond the mirror' with the intention of discovering more of your intrinsic power and beauty. That requires a shift of perception. So I invite you to change the glasses you view life through and take a closer, more loving look at yourself from a more generous perspective.

This book will take you on a journey that will help you expand your thoughts, while you open your heart. To truly honor your Soul, it is imperative you continue to stretch your vision of who you are and what is possible, by claiming your Soul's Legacy – the gifts that you were born with.

This book is set out in two parts. Part One explains the key principles used throughout the program. You will need to understand the different aspects of your nature, and how you specifically create your reality, before you begin the transformation process. Part One offers you the insight, knowledge and wisdom you will need to claim more of the power and beauty of your Soul.

Part Two provides you with the practical tools and guidance necessary to help you track the Destiny Points in the Map of your Soul that chart a course towards your Optimum Future Self. Along the way, you will uncover your Soul Contracts with the angels, allies and adversaries who appear in your life to help you learn your Life's Lessons. This will allow you to gather clues that ultimately reveal your Soul's Purpose and help you discover your true Destiny.

PART ONE

The Map of the Soul

Uncovering the Truth – The Basic Principles

Allies on Your Journey–
Your Inner Self
The Majesty of your Soul

'The beauty and majesty of your Soul is incomparable. It is the one thing that remains untarnished and constant in a world that is fraught with challenge.'

Prior to entering the physical world, you were originally one with God/Goddess/All That Is or the Source. You were a spark of consciousness – a spark of light and a piece of love with no identity. You split off from Oneness to find yourself. By taking on an individual identity, as a reflection of your Soul, you remain separate from the whole and have the opportunity to recognize your uniqueness. You are an aspect of God, and as you grow, you are becoming more so.

God/Goddess/All That Is, as infinite love, is constantly expanding and seeking more of itself. Living as a microcosm within the macrocosm, you are constantly searching and stretching to perceive more of your true potential, which is where your growth begins. Your Higher Self or Higher

Consciousness is an exalted part of you seeking to grow as an aspect of your Soul. Your Higher Self guides your journey, from your original separation until you consciously choose to return to Source, to God/Goddess/All That Is, to Love. That is the journey of returning home – and that is your spiritual heritage.

As an aspect of God, you are a creator in your own right. You have the power to generate your reality with your individual thoughts, which sparks creation. Everything in your reality is a reflection of your thoughts, just as you are a thought in the mind of God. In essence, you are united with the Goddess – the Source of Love and Creation. Your love has the power to sustain life.

Although we pretend to be separate, we will never be separate. Enlightenment is about ending that pretence and remembering who we are. Your ultimate destiny is to move towards unity and oneness, claiming the majesty of your Soul. In truth, your Soul is one with the Source. There is no separation other than the boundaries you construct with your mind, with your Ego.

Your Soul is a living, vibrant being that exists at the heart of your essence. It is the substance from which your identity emerges. Your Soul is the essence of who you are, throughout a multitude of lifetimes, beyond and through the sands of time. It was with you from the moment of your birth; it will be with you until your death and it remains with you during your passage in-between.

When your Soul originally separated from God/Goddess/All That Is or The Source, it refracted itself into different rays of experience, as forms of consciousness. Your Soul incarnates to experience life through a series of incarnations within which your physical body is unique. Each aspect of your Soul operates as a part of the whole in a complex, highly synchronized manner.

Although the physical body is governed by time and space – your Soul exists beyond the third dimension. It operates beyond time and space and has no linear dynamics to it. All that is experienced by your Soul, no matter what level or dimension it functions in, occurs simultaneously. It is the expansion of consciousness, desiring to experience more of itself. All the while, it remains a constant source of love and inspiration.

Your Soul is the aspect of your being that observes life through your inner senses. A lens to perceive life beyond the limits of your familiar five senses – through frequencies of vibration. To perceive the invisible side of life, you need to alter your measuring and calibrating devices. It is not sufficient to merely see with your physical eyes or hear with your ears or touch with your skin and smell with your nose. You need to use more than your five familiar senses and reawaken your unfamiliar senses. To do this you need to approach the world with a 'beginner's mind', as if you are seeing things for the very first time – in a state of innocence.

Your Soul is the means through which you perceive or sense the Essence of Life or All That Is, and the lens through which God/Goddess/All That Is perceives you. Your sensory system is capable of functioning on many different levels. As you expand your awareness and alter your measuring and calibrating devices, you can perceive more of your reality. During that process you refine or hone your sensory system or your sixth sense, allowing yourself to experience what exists beyond the world that you know.

Imagination is the key and is the gateway to your inner senses. You allow images to impress your mind and feelings; in the same way you do in dreams. You sense the light of something or someone, which is the Spirit. Similarly with the sense of substance or life – which is Soul. The light is coded with information that is communicated through the unspoken word. You don't hear a voice; you sense a presence that has no words and is registered as an imprint. Opening this gateway allows you to be more conscious of others. To sense the life, the light, and the voice within them and not just view them physically.

Your Soul is a portal or gateway. It remains unseen because it has no form or boundaries, yet it is there to be imagined and will use the form you imagine it to be as a way to reach you. Your Soul is pure energy or consciousness without a body – it is a doorway through which you can be touched and moved in the depth of feeling. Beyond the illusion of separateness you are one.

By engaging with your Soul with greater substance, you can gain power through an experience. You are always either knowingly or unknowingly in pursuit of more love and greater freedom and your Soul seeks power through experience. When you guard and defend yourself from what you don't want to experience you no longer receive from life gracefully. Your Soul holds the space for you to be full, bountiful and prosperous. Not as a way of separating you from others but as a way of you becoming more of who you really are, with the freedom to be more of your True Self.

The general consensus has reduced the Soul to myth. Therefore, the Soul reaches us the only way it can. Your Soul speaks to you in the silence and in the stillness. It offers its gifts through enchanted moments and through the crises of your life. It communicates all the information you need to know through captivating wisdom. The voice of your Soul is not vocalized; it doesn't have words. The Soul communicates through imagination and speaks in pictures, sending subtle messages through dreams, visions and intuition.

There are several ways that you can engage with your Soul or experience more of its presence. The first and most common way is to connect with nature. To enter the silence with the aim of sensing the sublime beauty that exists within the essence of all life, allowing yourself to be inspired or moved. It can be as simple as watching a sunset or walking through the woods. The key is to stay fully present in the moment while you remain receptive to being 'impressed'. Those sacred moments where the beauty of nature is palpable call us to be in awe of the majesty of creation and remind us that life is a gift.

Another way to presence your Soul is through gentleness or entering a state of 'gentle repose'. Your Soul responds to tenderness – a receptive state where you align with innocence. During those times you place your Ego aside and approach the world with an open heart and clear mind, accessing goodness, truth and beauty.

You also engage with your Soul by experiencing 'the sweet sorrow' that is associated with loss – a loss that calls you to feel deeper compassion and greater love. Then there is joy. Our Soul resides in a sea of joy – in a state of constant harmony with the universe. Opening to joy is a powerful way to connect with your Soul and augment your creativity. Joy has the capacity to add dimension to your dreams and awaken your innocence, aligning you with optimal futures. In each of these states you presence more of your Soul and can embrace the love that is beyond all names.

Your Soul is always with you and becomes detectable when you raise your emotional resonance. It will work with you but it has its own plane and therefore will never be fully understood.

The Wonder
of your Spirit

'Perceiving life through the eyes of a child, through the eyes of innocence, is the key to connecting with your Soul and awakening more of your Spirit. Life is an adventure and your world is a playground waiting to be explored.'

Your Soul, as the feminine side of your nature, perceives and conceives. It grounds itself in your physical body giving birth to your Spirit, which is masculine energy. Your Spirit is the fire, the light and the breath of you. It enters the fetus at various times from the point of conception, at the time of birth, or slightly after birth. As a portal, your Soul motivates the dynamics of doing – Spirit is active, always stretching to seek more light. Soul, being feminine, waits to be found; while Spirit searches for deeper meaning and understanding as it seeks to discover more of itself and the world it lives in.

We are all learning to reconnect with our Soul, through our inner senses, with the underlying compulsion to fulfill our ultimate destiny. At that point we will each become autonomous, living in a state of love, joy, individuality and freedom.

However conscious or yet to become conscious you are, you are already in that process of evolution. Wherever you are on your journey, by responding to the call of your Soul you can awaken more of your power, strengths, and talents to achieve and fulfill more of your potential. Your growth is accelerated by your desire and willingness to respond to your Soul's calling – a call to adventure. By evoking more of your passion, you can be filled and overflowing with the love and light of your Soul and Spirit.

Your Spirit is beyond matter or the third dimension, and yet it still has form. You emerge from the Oneness yet your Spirit is distinct, and in each incarnation your Spirit is unique. Your uniqueness is something to celebrate and is grounded by a sense of belonging – a feeling of aliveness and a sense of connectedness. The harmonious dance of Soul and Spirit allows your creativity and productivity to take on a whole new dimension. Your life is infused with joy and a depth of meaning and value.

When Soul and Spirit work together in harmonious accord, a self-sustaining, self-perpetuating magic is set in motion and you gain power through experience. The masculine and feminine sides of your nature are then beautifully balanced. You call upon the wisdom of your Soul and the freedom of your Spirit to awaken more of your True Self.

The Beauty of your Higher Self

'Your Higher Self is always with you, gently calling you to acknowledge the greater parts of yourselves. Fostering that relationship will allow you to be inspired by wisdom and nourished by love.'

The higher aspects of your consciousness exist in the realm of the unconscious. Your Higher Self is the guardian that holds all the information in your conscious and subconscious minds and in the unconscious – it is the keeper of all the possibilities of who you are and who you are becoming.

During those times that you sense you are greater than you know, you become aware of your Higher Self with its immense love and power. Your Higher Self is always with you as your constant companion and ally on your path to self-realization, loving you unconditionally as you expand your vision of who you are and what is possible.

In each incarnation, your Higher Self is a unique part of your nature. In its anthropomorphic form, it is the same sex as you with similar features – untainted by the negativity that presents itself in the physical world. You can connect with your Higher Self in meditation, by using that image as a means to deepen your relationship.

When you were a very young child, before your Ego and rational mind were fully developed, your sensitivity levels were far more heightened. You were naturally in touch with your inner senses, using your imagination and feelings to explore and experience life. Rather than forming rigid beliefs about your world and identity, you were in a state of innocence, allowing yourself to be impressed by the mysterious, magical side of life.

As an adult, that subtle, yet powerful aspect of your nature is often overshadowed by your logical thoughts and the strength of your will. When that imbalance occurs, it is easy to dismiss your intuition and the greater parts of yourself. By re-learning to trust the receptive side of your nature, in the same way you did as a child, you can begin to remember your true heritage and experience what exists beyond the world that you know.

Love is your natural state of being and is always available to you. Although there are times when you may feel alienated and uncertain, you are never really alone. Those feelings of being separate are founded on the boundaries you create with your conscious mind, kept in place by the constructs of your Ego.

Taking quiet time in contemplation and meditation will create an avenue for your Higher Self and Soul to communicate with you through your intuition. The way you deepen your connection is through your imagination and feelings – the language of your subconscious self. Entering a fully receptive state, you open up to being 'impressed' through your imagination. The communication is detected through your inner senses – as feelings, symbols or images. The key is to empty your mind and allow the information to come to you rather than forcing an outcome.

Using your subconscious as your go-between, you can receive direct guidance and inspiration. The art of interpreting those messages takes practice, patience and thoughtful consideration. Eventually you will decipher the information almost spontaneously.

The Power of your Subconscious

'Forming an alliance with your subconscious, you can access the depths of your untapped resources. It knows no difference between the physical world and the world of your dreams and imagination. Like a faithful servant, it delivers whatever you request in partnership with your Soul.'

Your subconscious self operates in the fourth dimension where time and space don't exist. It is your gateway to the unconscious. As the intermediary between your conscious mind and the unconscious, your subconscious acts as a faithful servant that will deliver anything you request. It knows no difference between what you imagine and what you perceive in the physical world.

Your subconscious self takes instruction through your consistent thoughts, which are backed by feelings and images. It holds the complete memory of the sum total of all of your experiences and is the keeper of your core beliefs. Because your subconscious beliefs are like a magnet that attracts the events that happen in your world, you have the choice of either consciously creating your reality or subconsciously allowing things to occur. You will continue to attract similar events and experiences until you alter the way you think and feel or change your beliefs. This is the way you ultimately re-program your subconscious mind and alter the course of your destiny.

You are the custodian and caretaker of your Soul. Therefore the quality of the relationship you have with yourself is paramount. How you feel about yourself and how you view your potential is extremely important – it is the basis of what you ultimately create. Your subconscious has gradually formed an image of who you are, which you project into the physical world. Your internal self-image dictates exactly what you attract and determines what is possible.

If you consistently and consciously expand your internal self-image, your subconscious will take the new program and filter it through into your physical reality, in the form of opportunities. It is then up to you to choose which direction to take, based on your will.

What you receive from life is not based on what you deserve, it is based on how much you are willing to receive.

The Journey of your Soul

'Your Soul is multidimensional by nature –
it exists in multiple places and times, constantly
seeking new and creative experiences. Your
known physical universe is only one of an
infinite array of many; you live through
numerous lifetimes in different states
of consciousness.'

To comprehend the journey of the Soul it is important to understand that time doesn't exist beyond the third dimension. Einstein and other scientists have proven that time is an illusion. In the fourth dimension and beyond, time doesn't exist. It is a construct we have developed to create order in the chaos. The future and past are all happening simultaneously. Your future selves already exist along with your past selves – each a counterpart of your Soul and Spirit, alive and individual at one time.

It is the same with reincarnation. When most people think of reincarnation, they think of linear progression as the Soul perfects itself in succeeding lifetimes. Your Soul is constantly in the process of expanding through numerous lifetimes – each with a primary Life Focus or Soul's

Purpose. In each lifetime, there are endless varieties of this theme – far too many for us to fathom.

Suffice to say that your Soul has infinite potential and you have the ability to tap into that reservoir when you move beyond the constraints of your logical thoughts to explore the unconscious.

When we pick up anything on a psychic level it is through the Akasha, which is the ether that permeates everything in the universe. It acts as the agent through which electromagnetic forces operate. The afterlife co-exists within the world we live in; on a subtler dimension in the unconscious. It is through our subconscious mind that we access other dimensions, registering pictures and feelings through our inner senses.

From a quantum perspective, you are pure energy. Everything in the universe is made up of light particles vibrating at a particular frequency. Those particles form streams of consciousness.

The best way to understand the concept of the multi-dimensional self is to consider the way a television operates. Radios and televisions receive and transmit signals. Each network broadcasts its programs on a particular bandwidth using electromagnetic waves. Whenever you change channels on a remote control you tune into a different frequency, which alters the station and program you view. As you change from one channel to the next, you can view a drama, a comedy or suspenseful thriller by simply shifting your point of focus. There may be 250 television shows running at the same time, yet you only fully experience the one that has your complete attention.

All of your probable and possible selves – past and future, are different representations of your Soul. Each of your possible selves vibrates at a different frequency of light. You are merely shifting your focus from one reality to the next in the same way you do when you are asleep and dreaming. During those periods your logical mind is put to rest and you enter the fourth dimension and the world of your subconscious. It is through your subconscious that you access the unconscious – the realm of the multi-dimensional self.

Your Soul's Blueprint

'Your Soul's Blueprint is made of a myriad of interwoven possibilities and probabilities. We choose our strengths, talents and life's lessons before entering our body – but what we do with those characteristics is never predetermined.'

Before you entered the physical world, you chose specific circumstances to set the stage for your spiritual growth. Your Soul's Blueprint encompasses everything you need to help you learn your life's lessons. In many ways, that blueprint can be looked upon as your 'spiritual DNA'.

On a Soul level, you chose your primary relationships, time and place of birth and inherent talents. You created Soul Contracts, particularly with your parents, which allowed you to adopt certain beliefs, attitudes and images. Those key components form the 'positive and negative scripts' you live on a daily basis, which attract certain experiences into your world. They create the fabric of the Dark and Light Matrix of your Soul's Hologram – a web of intricate patterns comprised of your possible selves.

Your spiritual DNA is encoded within the matrix of your Soul's Hologram. That divine blueprint is set in place to help you develop your strengths, nurture your talents and sharpen your skills. You were born with gifts and talents waiting to be discovered. Like buried treasure, they remain within your unconscious until you are willing to claim them.

When you made the choice to incarnate as an aspect of your Soul's identity, a specific field of energy was created that records each and every one of your experiences. That information is held in the Akashic records. Each Soul's record has a unique frequency, like a fingerprint, that exists within the energy field of the universe. Every thought, word, and deed of each Soul, who has lived throughout history, is stored in that central storehouse which connects each one of us energetically in the unified field.

These records are impressed on Akasha, which can also be called Somniferous Ether. By tuning into that network, psychics can detect past, present and future events, which are encoded in the field.

Each possibility is like an energetic thread that is impressed with information. Like a television signal, it correlates with a distinct band of frequency that has a particular resonance. The threads, or streams of consciousness, form a matrix, which is similar in concept to DNA.

Our biological DNA is like a thumbprint. Our ancestral genes set up a predisposition toward certain physical characteristics and traits, which correlate with our life's lessons and Soul's Purpose. The DNA sequence specifies the exact genetic instructions required to create our strengths and weaknesses and are coded with information that makes each of us unique.

Every cell in our body has the same DNA that holds many dimensions of information in a subtle network of interacting frequencies. It contains defined patterns or threadlike 'packages' – a set of chromosomes that are the inheritable traits or signatures in the nucleus of the cells.

The legacy you received from your personal benefactors can be changed. On a Soul level, you chose your biological DNA as a means to develop your character – both physiologically and spiritually. You can transform the energies and forces of the legacy you received from your guardians regarding love, power and creativity. When you are willing to claim more of your spiritual heritage, by dismantling the Dark Matrix in your Soul's Hologram, you can live a far more rewarding and much more meaningful life.

The Dark and Light Matrix

The Dark Matrix

Your Dark Matrix is made up of a network of behavior patterns that spring from the sum total of your negative beliefs and images – held in place by a construct of restrictive emotions such as guilt, fear, shame, loneliness and despair. It contains the vestiges of your past, relating to self-sabotage, self-punishment, lack of deserving and your denial of love. It exists within the very patterns of your brain and within the chemistry of your body in the matrix of the double helix of your DNA.

Your Dark Matrix is a shield you created in your childhood to protect you in a world that at times seemed unjust and intimidating. It was compounded somewhere in your adolescence when the wounds of life extinguished the fire of your Spirit and you felt abandoned by your Soul. You created a fortress, which protected you from further hurt and played a role in making you safe. Although it offered you a form of protection, it also created a prison that restricted your freedom and held you captive.

The Dark Matrix continues to exert its debilitating, imprisoning force until you claim more of your True Self and align your energy with love, joy, individuality and freedom. To genuinely dismantle the Dark Matrix, it is important you understand the nature and impact of your limiting beliefs, your addictions, blockages and payoffs, and the negative contracts and scripts you abide by.

Your power to transcend the Dark Matrix rests on claiming your right to use your destiny to consciously direct your evolution. Part of your Soul's Purpose is to draw on your power to create your own reality as you move toward complete authority and freedom.

You are here to celebrate your love and creativity, embracing the depths of your goodness, truth and beauty. Part of that process is practicing forgiveness and self-acceptance. This happens by mastering your Ego and forming an intimate, loving relationship with your Higher Self, which eradicates karma.

The word karma is derived from Sanskrit 'kri', meaning 'to do or act out'. In Indian philosophies it is the 'action or deed', which causes the entire cycle of cause and effect. Through the law of karma, the effects of our deeds actively create our past, present, and future experiences.

Contrary to what many people believe, there is no 'Karma Lord' who inflicts karma on us, and there is no such thing as Karmic Law. We choose our own karma and at any given point we are free to change it. It is important that we recognize karma relates to choice: it is not a law.

Karma is the backdrop behind all our lifetimes as we evolve towards unity and oneness. All things are simultaneous. We are responsible for our own life, including the joy or sorrow it brings to others and ourselves.

The Light Matrix

Your Light Matrix is made up of your fortune. It is an invisible force or energy at play that determines the events of your life. Good fortune is your fate – your destiny. Yet, destiny goes hand in hand with the fact that you create your own reality. Your fate is determined by the fundamental choices you make. You are the one who determines the events in your life. Those invisible forces of fate and destiny can be directed; not controlled but directed.

Your fortune emerges out of your talent – those gifts given to you before you incarnate. They enable you to form your divine destiny, which is always positive. Your destiny is not only a mysterious gift given to you; it is a powerful force that you create.

Negativity is a product of the conscious mind and not Higher Consciousness. In our duality, we experience energy that is positive and therefore we create the balance of negativity. You develop 'bad fortune' when you don't use your strengths and power to allow your destiny to emerge from the Light Matrix.

Your talent is a gift given to you by God/Goddess/All That Is and your destiny is both given and self created.

The Light Matrix becomes visible through your strengths, power and talent. You find your good fortune by developing your relationship with abundance – which begins with discovering and sharing the bounty of your inner-self. Your Optimum Future Self already exists as a living, breathing part of creation. You align with its resonance when you embrace the things that spark your passion – the things that trigger your boundless love and unbridled enthusiasm. It is simply a matter of shifting the way you perceive yourself and life.

Although the Dark and Light Matrix are associated with your destiny, fate works with destiny and you choose your destiny. It is a resonance made up of the choices you have made long ago on a Soul level, along with your biological heritage.

However, when it comes to the Soul's Blueprint, there are no absolutes and nothing is carved in stone – there are an infinite number of possibilities. We are all born with particular strengths and talents, yet it is our choice whether we use them. Although we may feel challenged by our inadequacies at times, we all have what it takes to succeed.

Your Soul's Blueprint contains a complex network of possibilities, connected at various milestones in your destiny. Those important events are Destiny Points, which turn the wheel of fortune. They appear as crossroads on the Map of the Soul, compelling you to make substantial choices that influence the course of your fate.

Those events give birth to beliefs, personality traits and patterns of behavior that have previously lain dormant. They are flagged as the defining moments you chose before you were born which shape your spiritual growth. The Destiny Points are triggered by the emotional exchange in your key relationships, whether that exchange resulted in emotional trauma or inspired spirited passion.

Soul Contracts are formed with the significant people in our lives and unfold according to the framework of our core beliefs. The 'players' who appear on the stage of your life show up as either angels or demons with the purpose of fostering your growth. No matter what form they take, they are ultimately there to help us establish our strengths, which we eventually use to conquer our weaknesses and claim more of our True Self.

No matter how distressing your life circumstances can appear, there is always someone waiting in the wings to help you traverse the next part of your Soul's journey and assist you with your growth by shining a light on your true potential.

Although there are many lessons you are here to learn, there is one primary lesson that highlights your Soul's Purpose and your life focus. Your primary lesson supports every other lesson and weaves itself through both your Dark and Light Matrix. The challenges that your life presents allows you to claim more of your strengths as you discover the power and beauty of your Soul, helping you align with your optimal futures.

The way you shift from one probability to the next is by shifting your resonance. The resonance or field of energy that determines your fate can be changed. It can shift as you improve the quality of your thoughts and feelings and, as a consequence, alter your choices. Part of your destiny is to dismantle the Dark Matrix in your Soul's Hologram so you can lift into the higher frequencies of love, joy, individuality and freedom – the magnetic field associated with the Light Matrix.

We are all born with the seeds of greatness. When you came into this world, you brought with you the attributes needed to support you as a completely self-expressed, whole and complete individual. When your passion or interest is sparked in a particular area, this serves as a clue to your inherent talents. If you love anything in this world it will bring you closer to joy and the joy you experience will bring you closer to your Soul.

Your intuition and imagination will serve as a guide to help you uncover your full potential. That will enable you to create and live out a dream that is inspired by your heart.

Dominion –
the Divine Truth

'In a state of Dominion you maintain a conscious, co-creative relationship with God/Goddess/All That Is. You choose to be giving and loving while you remain receptive to being loved.'

Living in a state of dominion, you embrace the fact that life is a gift to be enjoyed, knowing you live in a gracious, welcoming world that is filled with love and abundance. You view the world as a living consciousness that supports the harmonious dance of your Soul and Spirit and celebrates your existence. In this position the world becomes a place in which to play.

Entering this exalted state allows you to use your creativity in co-creative relationship with God/Goddess/All That Is. It supports the principle of unity and oneness, fostering the greatest good of all. You share the bounty of All That Is, using those resources to create with your Higher Self and Soul. You form an inner alliance between the different parts of you – the magical child, the curious adolescent and the spiritual adult, knowing you are responsible for creating your own reality. Feeling in your power as a co-creator, you stand tall, humbly knowing your intrinsic worth.

The World of Dominion is based on generously giving and accepting rather than fearing and blaming. Being emotionally free from the old patterns of the past – consciously creating your future rather than continually fixing what's wrong. Dominion is linked to your personal power – gaining power through an experience rather than using domination, intimidation or manipulation through weakness to get what you want out of life. Without the willingness and ability to operate in dominion, it is impossible to genuinely connect with your Higher Self.

Dominion exists in the field of love. You have to be willing to perceive and conceive of that world before you see it – if you change your attitude your world will reflect something different. Your power comes from your willingness to act and create – to use your imagination as a reference for what is possible and not rely on the measures of your past.

You knew dominion as a young child when you were in a state of innocence. It is a state you are returning to by giving up your need to control. When you operate from a place of control, love no longer exists in the space. You choose either one or the other – love or control.

There is also a future you living in a state of dominion beyond the parameters of time and space. The steps to getting there are embracing the qualities of your future self, who is already there.

To stay on track, assess and re-assess where you are coming from. Are you controlling or allowing, being receptive or stubbornly resisting being loved? Are you accepting responsibility as the creator of your reality or are you blaming circumstances, yourself or others for not having what you want? Dominion upholds the Divine Truth, which supports a world of love, joy, individuality and freedom.

The Divine Truth:

1. Your point of power exists in the moment.
2. You were born with the power to create your own reality and determine the course of your destiny. You either consciously create your reality, or subconsciously allow events to take place in your world.
3. What you create in your physical world is a reflection of your own beliefs.
4. To experience love and freedom, you have to be willing to give up control.
5. You have free will.
6. You are whole and complete – there is nothing missing inside of you.
7. You live in a world filled with love, abundance and joy. The way you perceive your world determines your experience.
8. What you receive is based on what you are willing to have and not on what you deserve.
9. Life is a gift from God/Goddess/All That Is and you are here to learn to receive.
10. The physical world is an illusion – so you can have as much of the illusion as you like.
11. You are a part of the process of evolution – you are who you are becoming and not just who you have been.
12. You can be anyone, have anything and do anything you choose, with harm to none.

Keep in mind that living in a Dominion supports the principle of unity and oneness where peace and harmony prevail. This state, which is our natural state, fosters the greatest good of all. No harm can come to any of us unless we lose sight of our true worth. There are no victims in this world; there are only poor or limiting choices. You are inherently entitled to receive the bounty of life and love without struggle, force, manipulation or control in a way that contributes to rather than harms others.

Adversaries
on your Journey–
Your Ego
The Nature of Ego

'The negative side of the Ego has only two perspectives – being better than or less than others, but never equal to. It creates far too much separation, often resulting in fear, alienation and loneliness.'

On a deeper, spiritual level we are all one. The ultimate purpose of your Ego is to create healthy boundaries that allow you to have a unique identity in the physical world, as an intricate part of All That Is.

Your self-confidence springs from your ability to depend on your internal resources and maintain a positively functioning Ego.

Your personal power as a unique being comes from your estimation of who you are and what you can achieve. Your self-esteem relies on your ability to cope, based on your levels of trust, hope, humility and courage.

The original intention of Ego was to be your assistant. Its sole objective was to retrieve information from the outside world for you to evaluate and interpret.

You were not born with a negative Ego. It became negative when its growth was arrested during your infancy, childhood or during your adolescence. That happens because we are not taught to value our intuition and honor our spiritual heritage. Because of our self-doubt, we become susceptible to believing that we are powerless in certain areas and lose sight of our intrinsic worth. Feeling overwhelmed, we rely on our Ego to get us what we want.

At some point during your development, you were unwilling or unable to heal and mature your Ego and it developed a destructive side to its nature. You then unconsciously gave your Ego permission to interpret the information you received from the outside world, forfeiting that responsibility. The negative side of the Ego will always leave you in a position of feeling better than or less than others, but never equal to them. It creates trenches of separation and breeds co-dependence, rather than co-operation and accord. Ego seeks power by trying to control people, circumstances and experiences – it seeks power over.

The negative side of your Ego can destroy in minutes what it has taken you years to build. It erodes trust, overshadows love, and leads to self-betrayal.

Your Ego is not the enemy, but your negative Ego is. It lies, cheats and exaggerates with a penchant for control. With your Higher Self and Soul as your allies, embellish your world with goodness, truth and beauty.

Whenever you evaluate yourself as being superior or inferior to anyone else, just remember your Ego's leading the way. It is the part of your conscious mind that is responsible for negative self-talk. It rears its head as the judge, the critic, and the inner tyrant that drives you toward self-punishment. It thrives on competition and making comparisons, which basically negates your uniqueness.

Allowing your Ego to interpret the information that comes to you from the outside world will trip you up and sabotage your relationships – all the while planting seeds of doubt. The solution is not to kill your negative Ego but to mature it and build a positive one.

The Inner Critic

'This voice of Ego will always lead us to fear, anxiety, confusion and doubt. We have the choice of either honoring our feelings or falling asleep and letting our Ego take control.'

The internal critic can be very subtle or blatantly obvious. At times it tells us that we are weak, hopeless, ugly, powerless or stupid. On other days, the Ego will inappropriately inform us that we are invincible, infallible and are sublimely superior. Those comments about your limitations and your eminence need to be challenged immediately or they will destroy the equality and harmony in your relationships.

The Ego looks for your Achilles' heel and grinds away until you're defeated. So be very conscious of the negative voice within you, and when it starts to wear you down or erode your confidence – just pull the plug! Don't argue with it, or even try and reason with it – nip it in the bud.

Everyone you meet will have an opinion about you and unless their opinion is free of judgment and criticism, it springs from negative Ego. If you look to someone else to determine your worth, you are setting yourself up to be crucified.

Does this mean you shouldn't listen to other people's feedback? Not necessarily. If a person is generous and objective in their appraisal, they are usually worth listening to. If they were motivated by Ego, you would be wise to bypass their comments.

Although you're likely to take other people's criticism seriously, and are well aware that judgment hurts, you can often be ignorant to the degree of impact your negative thoughts have on your own feelings. If you remain sensitive to your feelings and pay attention to your internal dialogue, you will eventually recognize you have the power to change your emotional experience.

The Inner Tyrant

'It is easy to become trapped in a downward spiral of seeking approval and outside validation. When you give your power away, it often leads to addiction and various forms of self-punishment.'

Your choices need to empower you to grow, rather than deplete your energy. If you continue to take negative options, you simply deny yourself the right to succeed and enjoy a full life. If you repress your feelings and compromise your choices, it is a sign you have fallen prey to your negative beliefs. On some level you don't genuinely believe you deserve to have what you truly desire. Chances are you will reach for something to mask the pain, which often leads to self-punishment.

The desire we have to punish ourselves can be incredibly subtle. If you look at the choices you make on a daily basis, you will gauge precisely how much you care about yourself.

No matter what form the addiction takes, whether it is food, alcohol, drugs or excessive amounts of sex, work or even television – if it creates imbalance, it is a form of self-punishment. Beneath any addiction lies a sense of powerlessness and fear. Opting for the quick fix and the easy way out will only lead to further distress.

Self-punishment, addiction and self-pity are a result of feelings of unworthiness, founded on restrictive core beliefs. If you are not living a life that truly nourishes and inspires you, you have fallen prey to the antics of your Ego. Feeling genuinely compassionate toward yourself is what alters negative behavior – not self-pity but compassion.

Self-pity springs from Ego and is used as a way of manipulating, whereas compassion is aligned with love and brings you in touch with your Soul and Higher Self.

Victims and martyrs not only end up hurting themselves, they end up hurting others. Unless the Ego is disempowered, the vicious cycle remains in place and the punishment simply continues.

If you don't challenge your compulsive thoughts, you will simply continue to override your feelings and struggle to gain control. At the end of the day you are the caretaker and custodian of your heart and your feelings connect you directly with your Soul. It is essential you align your choices with love and expansion and not instant gratification. If you surrender to your Ego, it will keep you feeling trapped and powerless.

Your choices will either empower or imprison you. If you set your intention to stay humble and receptive, and then pay attention to where your thoughts are going, you will develop the skill of remaining peaceful and centered. The more you practice, the greater the benefits. Feeling better about your self is vitally important; you are more apt to make wiser decisions and far more generous choices.

Domination –
The Ego's Deception

'Domination is a state that reflects a desire to have power over. It separates you from love, freedom and joy. There is always an alternative route to get to the same destination; you simply have to expand your vision, stay receptive and be willing to give up control.'

When we choose to follow the deception and lies of the negative Ego we turn our back on the World of Dominion and enter the World of Domination – both as individuals and as a collective humanity.

Performance and appearances are often valued more than a person's essence. 'Looking good' takes precedence over feeling good. This is indicative of chauvinism, which exalts the masculine energy and represses the feminine. The World of Domination robs us of our spiritual heritage and throws us into struggle, limitation and alienation. It is characterized by fear, manipulation, intimidation, bullying, righteousness and control.

To break free of that paradigm, you need to be willing to give up your desire to control or manipulate your reality and move toward graceful co-creation.

You live in a world of duality where opposites exist as a part of the whole. As an adult you have single authority and freedom of choice. Ultimately all of your choices spring from two options – to align with fear and limitation or love and expansion.

Stay mindful and catch yourself when you are being deceived by the arrogance and chauvinism of your Ego. Being loved has nothing to do with your physical appearance, the capacity of your brain, your material status or the level of your performance. It has everything to do with your level of self-worth and just how much you're willing to receive.

If you are operating in the World of Domination, you are playing the role of being better than or less than others; supporting your Ego rather than building an alliance with your Soul and Spirit. Every choice or action you take, including your conversations, moves you closer to your Higher Self or nearer to your Ego. One motion contaminates your world and the other adds value and vitality – there is no middle ground.

Everything in creation is sustained by love. To consider yourself excluded from that equation is arrogance. Whenever you believe that you are not good enough, or you don't deserve what you desire, you justify that position. Your Ego will use those statements as an excuse to dominate. Whether you play out the role of victim, tyrant or noble martyr, you are still vying for power.

Following the Ego's reign, the world seems like a frightening place where you can often feel overly vulnerable or powerless. That sets up the pattern for judgment and blame and negates your responsibility as the creator of your reality.

Domination reinforces a belief that our resources are limited. The cruelty, greed, envy, jealousy and rage in the world are simply a reflection of fear and denial of love. Domination is aligned with taking – not giving; pushing and competing rather than graciously receiving.

There are times we all compete. Whether that is for recognition, for control, for space, for power or even for love; competition supports the belief that we live in a limited world where we have to struggle to be acknowledged and get what we want.

Identifying this pattern in our relationships can illustrate how destructive competitive behavior can be. It fosters whining and complaining rather than gratitude, humility, hope and trust which open us to love and receiving the gifts life has to offer.

PART TWO

Creating New Maps for the Future

Aligning with your Authentic Self

Logging the
Map of the Soul
The Basic Tools

**As you progress through the Twelve Levels
of Discovery, you will be asked to do a series
of exercises and keep a record of specific
insights called Key Coordinates.**

You will need to create two sections in your journal. The first section can
be used to do your exercises, record your findings and make notes on any
Soul-Speak.

Create a smaller section in the back of the journal for the Map of the
Soul Insights, which you will use to record your Key Coordinates.

Those insights lay the foundation for Discovering Your True Purpose.
That is why it is imperative that you do ALL of the exercises and do them
in sequence. They take you through a step-by-step process that will help
you create the Map of your Soul. You can then use that map to navigate

your way to the pinnacle point in your Soul's Hologram – a state of love, joy, individuality and freedom.

Along the way, you will define the components of your Dark Matrix, pinpointing your blockages and the reasons why you forfeit your personal power. The next step is to surmount those obstacles and strengthen your resources by claiming more of your True Self.

Following that trail, you will lift into the Light Matrix, reclaiming your personal power and uncovering more of Soul's Purpose.

It is absolutely crucial that you complete each of the exercises and log your discoveries before you move on.

Each of the Twelve Levels will provide you with the direction, support and inspiration you will need to keep up momentum while discovering your true purpose. Although I will guide you every step of the way, you will be ultimately working with your Higher Self and Soul and are responsible for your own success. At the end of the day you are the custodian and emissary for your Soul and Spirit in the physical world.

Every step you take toward developing your self-awareness will bring you reward. Just remember – anything worth achieving in this world takes effort. Self-mastery is achieved through perseverance.

When you reach Level 12, you will pull together all of the pieces of the puzzle to reveal your Soul's Purpose and your Optimum Future-Self. By this stage of the journey you will have founded a stronger connection to your Authentic Self and be able to distinguish when you are following 'True North'.

Soul-Speak – Your Soul's Whispers

Sensing your deepest feelings is the gauge to seeing if you are following your intuition and aligning with True North. When you are moving in a positive direction in life your emotions are buoyant. If you steer off course your feelings become constricted and your Soul will alert you through life's little whispers.

As you make your way through each of the Twelve Levels you will learn to interpret the language of your Soul or 'Soul-Speak' – a simple, yet powerful way to enter a co-creative relationship with your Higher Self. This will help you develop the perceptive, intuitive side of your nature, which will allow you to hear your Soul's call to adventure.

Intuition – Your Inner Compass

Your intuition is your means of knowing instinctively and directly, rather than through your rational mind and its conscious reasoning. Using your intuition allows you to gain access to a deeper source of wisdom by receiving guidance through your inner senses.

By allowing yourself to curtail your logical thoughts and attune to your inner self, you can gain a much more expansive view of what is available to you. It enables you to move beyond your preconceived ideas and allow yourself to be impressed by your Higher Self and Soul.

Developing your intuition takes practice. It takes discipline to still your thoughts and shift into sensing or feeling. The more you 'sense' rather than 'think', the stronger your intuition becomes.

It takes time and dedication to learn to successfully read your inner compass. Yet, rather than doing more, the challenge is honoring your feelings and being willing to trust them. The first step is to monitor the intensity of your will. When you are heading toward True North, your life is always graceful. If you go against the natural flow and push for control, things became a struggle.

The trick is to overcome your fears so they don't overshadow your genuine desires, and to stay receptive. It is important not to limit yourself by insisting things come from one particular source. That is merely a way of manipulating the illusion to force an outcome. Be humble enough to be open to all possibilities – that is the way miracles manifest.

Life-speak – Your World as a Mirror

Your Soul communicates through the cracks and crevices in your life, constantly sending you subtle 'whispers'. Those whispers offer guidance and also indicate if you are keeping your best interests at heart. Whenever you mindfully ask your Higher Self or Soul for deeper clarity or wisdom, regardless of the topic, the answers will always come. The key is to pay attention to the little signs that appear in your world. If you choose to turn a deaf ear to the whispers, your Soul will simply turn up the volume on the signs until you finally get the message. If you continue to overlook them, they will turn into 'shouts'.

Whether the clues are as subtle as a bird appearing regularly in your garden to remind you to enjoy life and sing, or as blatant as a succession of flat tires suggesting you stop to boost your morale, the whispers become increasingly more obvious.

Often the information can be more cryptic – broadcast via a newspaper headline, magazine article, movie or a television program. A song will even play on the radio at a time when the lyrics are uncannily relevant. Messages are delivered through a variety of means, including chance encounters with people. If three different friends over the course of a week recommended a particular book, the likelihood is it will contain the direction or clarity you've been seeking. These synchronistic occurrences are displays of 'life-speak'.

Keep in mind that what you manifest or attract into your world, including the quality of your relationships, is always a reflection of your core beliefs. If you are rear-ended in your car, you may subconsciously feel as though people are far too pushy or that you are at the mercy of other people's agendas. You will project things into your reality in order to gauge how far you have progressed or as feedback to show you where you need to change and grow.

The key is to respond by altering the way you perceive your life and see your true potential. Your world is a clear mirror on how much you are willing to receive and which parts of yourself you are willing to express and have acknowledged.

If you ignore the negativity in your world, the shouts will escalate and you will enter into a crisis. In a crisis you are unable to resume your normal routine and are compelled to review your circumstances and alter your behavior. This is your final 'wake up call'. If you refuse to stop and listen as that point, you will risk experiencing irretrievable loss – many a marriage has gone by the wayside because during a crisis one partner stubbornly refused to grow and change.

By consciously using 'life speak', your Soul will faithfully court you. Those very subtle messages that you are presented with on a daily basis can be very beautiful gifts.

Dream-speak – Your Inner Landscape

Whispers can also come to you from the inner world of dreams and visions. During sleep, you enter the realm of your subconscious – the custodian that gathers and stores content in your inner world. It gives you messages through symbols and images, highlighting your fears and aspirations and the areas where you are not at peace with the different parts of yourself.

Night dreams are often used for the purpose of teaching and healing in the fourth dimension, as you move beyond time and space you enter a world of pure possibility and probability and connect more deeply with your Soul.

The dreamscape is also the realm where your hopes, desires, fears and fantasies are revealed. You are free to test new ideas, find inspiration and seek resolution to many of the problems you face in the physical world.

Your future selves are already alive and past selves are still happening. All are parts of your Soul. Abilities that have been developed by your simultaneous selves can be tapped into and used in the dream state. Those gestalt experiences often show up in waking consciousness as ideas or intuitions, daydreams or visions. The dream realm provides a meeting ground for the various parts of you. So practice bringing your full waking consciousness into the dream state and you can experience lucid dreaming; the ability to meet different probable selves face-to-face, including those in other incarnations.

If you ask your subconscious to give you answers to specific questions before you go to sleep, it will deliver the information you request – as long as you are persistent. If you don't normally recall your dreams, repeatedly instruct your subconscious to remember until you do.

It helps to keep a pad and pen next to your bed as a declaration of intent to your subconscious. As soon as you wake up, even it is in the middle of the night, jot down notes. The key is not to fall back to sleep before you record the symbols. You will find that once you have been recording your dreams for a while, you will naturally remember.

There are also times where the answers you seek will appear during the course of the next day. Your subconscious will show you signs and messages by delivering the information through life speak in the physical world, so it appears in a framework you understand.

Remember that your subconscious mind is the intermediary between you and your Higher Self and Soul – a faithful servant that will deliver what you request. You can set your intention to work with your Higher Self during your sleep, by asking for assistance, inspiration or healing. To strengthen that alliance, be prepared to work in a co-creative relationship and stand in your power by being responsible, rather than asking to be rescued.

Body-speak – Your Physical Vehicle

Physical ailments are always a symptom of an underlying emotional cause. They are whispers from your Soul summoning your attention. As you learn and grow, there are inevitably times you will experience disappointment. Unfulfilled desires can leave you feeling deficient and plagued by self-doubt. Whenever you see yourself as powerless, flawed or unworthy of love, you perpetuate the cycle of pain. Stressful and suppressed emotional memories can store themselves in the body and eventually surface as illness or disease. Pain is our body's way of getting attention – not just from our minds but also from our hearts.

When physical ailments appear in your world, the volume of life-speak is dramatically increased. It is a warning to pay attention to suppressed emotions. At some point you have indicated to your subconscious that you are not willing to deal with the issue and so it buries the emotions in the unconscious. In the future, your Soul will seek a healing and the issue will then bubble up into the subconscious to be dealt with. Because you have previously instructed your subconscious to dismiss the emotions, as your faithful servant, it abides by your original request and rather than bring the issue to your conscious attention, it conveniently hides the pain in various locations of your body and it surfaces as imbalance.

Look for the specifics. Heart and chest conditions often relate to love and grief, stomach ailments to 'what you can't stomach' or digest, and throat problems to swallowed words, thoughts and feelings you are not willing to express. Look for the clues.

With eye problems – what don't you want to see? Who is a pain in the neck? What are you 'sick' or 'tired' of? To undergo a true healing, you need to not only attend to your body's needs but also acknowledge the emotional issues behind the physical manifestation.

Journaling

Keeping a daily journal is an incredibly powerful tool for self-discovery. Using your journal as a focal point, it will help you to clarify and explore your thoughts, emotions and beliefs so you can get in touch with your Authentic Self. It will give you an opportunity to view your life from a much broader and deeper perspective. To pinpoint what makes you happy in life and uncover the blockages that hinder your growth.

As you progress through to Level 12, you will be required to write in your journal on a daily basis. Consider it your trusty companion and friend as you undertake your quest to claim more of your True Self. You will use your journal as a means to build the relationship with your subconscious – the intermediary between your conscious mind and your Soul and Higher Self. Your aim is to create a co-creative relationship that will serve you for the rest of your life.

By using your journal to pull back and observe your thoughts, you can stay centered and become receptive to inner guidance, inspiration and wisdom; practicing the art of embracing stillness and learning to listen.

Journaling will allow you to stay peacefully detached, as you take on the position of the objective observer. Rather than consistently analyzing, formulating, judging and assessing, you can stay in touch with your feelings and be fully present. You can then process the information that comes from your world with a deeper understanding and from a much more expansive perspective. It will help you to naturally develop your perceptive abilities and intuition.

Once you get into the practice of considering the presence of your Higher Self, you will start to realize that life offers you abundant choices and a myriad of opportunities.

Your Soul will communicate with you through your subconscious and one of the most effective ways to receive counsel is through inspired writing. Taking the time to be still and allow your thoughts to flow onto paper will often help you get in touch with your deeper feelings. You can bypass your Ego and rational thoughts and allow your subconscious to take the lead.

Because your subconscious communicates through pictures, be receptive to symbols, spontaneous memories or visions that come to you through your imagination. They will ultimately help to guide you. Eventually you will learn how to interpret those images, as long as you are consistent.

Tracking your Soul's whispers or Soul-Speak in your daily journal will become a reliable method for you to gauge your progress and receive further direction. Part of that process is making note of life-speak – the signs that appear in your world on a daily basis to indicate whether you are still on course.

Both daydreams and night dreams can deliver messages from your Soul so throughout your journaling process you are encouraged to record them.

It is important that you take the time to sit and commune with the higher aspects of your consciousness, especially when you feel lost and confused. Journaling is a means to find your way back to the depths of your heart – in the gentleness.

When you were a very young child, before your Ego and rational mind started to develop, you were in a receptive state most of the time. You need to return to this state in order to remember your true heritage – a state of innocence. Although there are times when you may feel alienated and uncertain, you need to realize that you are never alone. There is no separation between you and the higher aspects of your consciousness – other than the boundaries you create with your conscious mind.

Journaling will help you move beyond your rational thoughts and reconnect with your essence.

Writing is an invaluable method of releasing denied or suppressed emotions, to free you up for new experiences. It will also help you gain greater insight and a deeper understanding of why certain things show up in your life. You can discover the hidden wisdom within all of your experiences and move to a point of peace and clarity.

Journaling supports you in reclaiming your power by highlighting the parts of you that have been denied or ignored, helping you to feel whole and complete. It is one of the best ways to nurture yourself, attend to your needs and acknowledge your preferences. Journaling is also a great way to log your insights, goals and aspirations.

Write with an open heart and an open mind and, above all, be honest. Otherwise you will only circumvent your growth and cheat yourself. It takes dedication and commitment to continue the process. Yet it is worth the effort it takes. You will probably find that after using your journal for a while you will look forward to that quiet time you have to be with yourself. It gives you a private space to turn your thoughts inward and simply reflect.

Most people get benefit from spending 20–30 minutes writing each day. The deeper you go, the more you will gain from the experience. Never wait until you feel like it – do it no matter how blocked you feel. Once you start writing it will free your energy up and you will move into the flow. Just go through the motions, and your emotions will respond once you are underway.

Don't control your thoughts; write whatever comes into your mind. Your discoveries need to be genuine, not contrived. A journal has nothing to do with good writing or grammar. It has everything to do with self-discovery. Don't try to compose or edit – just write. Watch your Ego: it may resist you doing this process. It will create all sorts of excuses why you shouldn't or don't need to do it.

Overcome your Ego by making a few brief notes on a piece of paper to begin to release your thoughts.

Trust the flow of your thoughts and feelings, no matter what comes up. Make certain you are feeling and not just thinking. Part of this process is you getting in touch with your inner self.

Be mindful of the times when you avoid writing in your journal because you don't want to deal with something uncomfortable. That is a good reason to persist. Remember one of your primary intentions is to face the fears and the issues you have refused to deal with. Growth and changing habits can sometimes be uncomfortable; you are learning to stretch. You will garner the rewards if you are consistent. That is what self-mastery is all about. It takes discipline and courage, which is the path to being extraordinary.

Affirmations

Using affirmations can be a powerful way of combating negative self-talk and altering limiting beliefs. Your life is a reflection of your beliefs, so unless you change your beliefs your life will remain the same.

Who you believe you are is at the base of your creation. You can chant a positive mantra all day long but unless that impacts the way you see yourself and the way that you genuinely feel about yourself, it will have no effect. It's your feelings and not just your mind that needs to be impressed.

During the times you feel emotionally challenged, declaring a clear, positive intention can shift your focus towards what you want to experience. These are the times you need to feed your subconscious with uplifting thoughts and images of who you ultimately wish to become. By declaring your intentions, and focusing your attention on what you want, you will eventually attract the experience. If you continue to give credence to what's missing, you will simply create more of the same. The key is to look to the future and not to use your past as a reference to what is possible.

There's one important thing to remember. Unless an affirmation is backed by strong emotions, and clear positive images, it will have no influence on your subconscious. Just one simple cameo of you living out your dreams, seen over and over again, is enough to prompt your subconscious to create new opportunities.

As you progress through each level of the course, it is important you hold a clear vision of your Optimum Future Self. Your subconscious is then given a definitive instruction on the possible futures to align with.

You are in the process of becoming more of your True Self. Therefore if you extend an affirmation by saying, 'I am and am becoming', you instruct your subconscious to expand your existing self-image and attract the experience. It demonstrates your right to choose. You can assert your authority to claim more of the intrinsic power and beauty of your Soul and Spirit.

Keeping up your momentum is crucial. By using your affirmations as a part of your daily routine, you continue to alter your perception of who you are becoming. Eventually that energy will shift your emotional resonance towards love, joy, individuality and freedom – aligning you with your Soul's Purpose and ultimate destiny.

Divine Truth and Key Word Contemplation

The importance of contemplating the Divine Truth and Key Words as you progress through each level is to examine and become conscious of where you give your power away. This will help you to determine where you stand strong and align with your Authentic Self or where you give your negative Ego permission to take control. Remember – responsibility equates with freedom.

Practicing the art of stilling your mind and taking quiet time in contemplation will create an avenue for your Higher Self and Soul to communicate through your intuition.

Using your subconscious as your go-between, you can receive direct guidance and allow an influx of inspiration. The key is to empty your mind and stay receptive, allowing the information to come to you. The communication is detected through your inner senses – your feelings and imagination.

As you progress through the twelve levels in Part Two of this book, you will be forming a co-creative relationship with your Higher Self and Soul, so it is important you accept mutual responsibility by continuing to expand your awareness. Because you are in charge of your thoughts and actions, it is essential that you either declare your intention or ask a question before you begin any introspective practice.

Your part is to be both assertive and receptive. That means you are open to enquiring and listening – allowing and responding – giving and receiving and, most importantly, loving and being loved. To strengthen your co-creative relationship, you need to be willing to learn to dance in harmony.

Becoming the Objective Observer

Entering a state of innocence allows you to operate from a place of acceptance rather than control or resistance. This enables you to become the 'Objective Observer'. You take a detached position, allowing things to be as they are, without reacting. Detachment has nothing to do with not caring; it means taking an impartial position where you remain receptive, rather than defensive.

There are two positions you can operate from in any given situation. You can either resist/react or allow/respond. The allow/respond approach enables you to take the role of the Objective Observer. Taking this position aligns you with your personal power while you expand your state of awareness. As an Objective Observer you choose to remain centered and perceive things from a higher vantage point, rather than struggle to gain control. That way you can use your intuitive senses and apply a more judicious form of reasoning.

It is quite easy to be an Objective Observer when looking at someone else's life. We are able to remain emotionally detached, yet take a considerate point of view, and be well aware of countless options. When it comes to our own lives however, we are often clouded by fear, which narrows our peripheral vision and numbs our intuition.

It is best to recognize and acknowledge your fears and then use your intuition to sense the best way to overcome obstacles. Taking that route enables you to stretch for deeper understanding and meaning, giving you an expansive view of what is possible. It will naturally bring you in touch with your Higher Self and help you to develop your sense of compassion. This is ultimately the way of the Objective Observer, which leads to greater wisdom and profound insights.

It is imperative you remain humble during this process. Pushing to gain resolution may work at times; yet it will leave you feeling exhausted. Accessing a state of innocence and becoming an Objective Observer is your key to experiencing love, joy, individuality and freedom.

Meditation

Meditation is a simple, practical way to clear your mind and enter a peaceful, receptive state. By stilling your thoughts, you can bypass the mechanics of logic and reason and connect more deeply with your intuitive senses.

During meditation your brain's activity alters significantly. Because there is less interference from your will, your emotional resonance shifts and your awareness moves beyond the third dimension of time and space.

Researchers at Harvard Medical School have used MRI technology, or Magnetic Resonance Imaging, to map the brain wave activity of meditating people and found that specific brain waves accompany various altered states of consciousness.

Meditating will help you to release negativity and expand your self-awareness, which is a crucial step toward discovering more of your True Self. That simple step toward self-realization will ultimately allow you to recognize the validity of your Soul – a primary source of love and the impetus of creation.

Once the routine is established, you will find the process is an invaluable way to strengthen your relationship with your Higher Self and Soul to stay centered during the course of your day.

By using your imagination to create your own internal sanctuary, you can establish a sacred space where you can gain access to feelings of love and unity. Practicing on a regular basis will help you to receive guidance, insight, inspiration and explore the depths of your own inner world.

It helps to set up a regular routine that you can stick to. Choose a comfortable place you won't be disturbed for at least 30 minutes. Sit in a relaxed position rather than lying down, to avoid falling asleep. You can review that situation at a later date when you are sure you can remain mindful. It is also a good idea to meditate first thing in the morning when your mind is refreshed.

Be patient with your process. It takes practice to still your thoughts. Eventually you will find that your subconscious will lead the way and you will naturally relax and drift into an altered state of consciousness.

The simple meditations provided in each level are based on creative visualization. They were designed to help you form a co-creative partnership with your subconscious.

Using images and feelings, you can plant new seeds in your subconscious mind, which will create opportunities for you to grow and heal. The meditations are an essential part of the program. By learning to strengthen your internal self-image, and change your core beliefs, you will shift your emotional resonance and align with the optimal futures in your Soul's Blueprint.

How to Prepare
for the Journey

It is imperative that you are fully committed to completing the program – it has been designed as a progressive course, so the best results occur only if you follow through all of the exercises laid out from Level 1 to Level 12. Your transformation is an ongoing process that continues to build as you expand your awareness.

The program is designed with the aim of taking you through the process of dismantling your Dark Matrix during the first six levels. This journey can be confronting, so keep in mind that when you get to Level 7 you will turn the corner and move into the Light Matrix. At some stage you reach a tipping point, where you have a significant breakthrough. Although you are likely to see results at the end of each level of the course, you can expect to see the full benefits when you reach Level 12 and navigate the Map of your Soul.

Unless you do the work, and do it earnestly, you cannot expect the results. If you want anything in your life to be different you need to change, and the only way we change is by letting go of the past and seeing ourselves from a more expanded point of view. So the next time you hear yourself complain about not feeling great, or missing out on something in life, you might want to remind yourself that you are the master of your own destiny and that you create your own fate.

One of the most, if not the most, important aspects of that process is learning to master your Ego. The negative side of your Ego is the part of you that feels like a talking parrot that sits on your shoulder and runs a constant commentary. You will find there are times when your Ego will resist doing the work and you will be plagued by the voice of doubt. It will tell you that 'you don't need to; why should you; that you couldn't be bothered; that you're too tired; that other people don't have to…' or, perhaps most deceptively, that you'll 'get to it later'.

On the worst day of all it will simply say, 'what's the point?' The point is this – unless you are willing to make an effort, no matter how small those steps may be, your life will never change. If you have heard yourself say 'yes but, I've tried' or 'yes but, what am I supposed to do?' or 'yes, but, what if it doesn't work?' just keep in mind the Ego often starts a sentence with 'yes but' or 'what if'. It is, after all, the voice of doubt.

So stop for a minute to review where you are coming from and be conscious of which voice is driving you. Ask yourself which part of you inspired you to pick up this book? Chances are it was your intuition or Higher Self. It was a Soul's whisper.

This is a great time for you to choose which voice you are going to follow – the voice of limitation and doubt or the voice of your Higher Self that leads you towards freedom.

Throughout the rest of the book I will remind you to keep considering 'where you are coming from' whenever you make your choices. Every choice and decision you make in your life is based on how you see yourself and who you believe you are.

It is my primary intention, throughout the course, to help you expand your perception of who you are and transcend your limiting beliefs.

Once you start answering the questions in each of the exercises there is a good chance you will feel confronted. Please keep in mind that at times we become 'comfortably numb' and being stirred from that sleep can be uncomfortable.

The aim of the process is to awaken more of your sleeping Soul and align you with your Authentic Self. That takes courage, trust and a willingness to change.

During the exercises don't suppress or deny your feelings. You are moving through a process of healing the past so you can chart a new course for the future. Remember what's at stake – love, joy, individuality and freedom.

Setting your Intention

To achieve your desired result it is important that you commit to an Agreement of Intent. Make a pledge to your Higher Self and Soul, not just yourself, as this way you'll realize it is a promise that deserves respect.

When you are ready, complete the following and note it in your Journal.

Agreement of Intent

I, _____ promise to:

Deepen the relationship I have with myself and to presence more of my Soul.

Commit to following through and completing all of the exercises as I progress from Level 1 to Level 12 considering my highest good.

Answer and enquire earnestly and honestly into the topic for each level of the course.

Be gentle with myself throughout the process, understanding that I am stretching myself beyond my limits, which may at times be challenging.

My heart's desires are:

_____

_____

_____

_____

_____

_____

_____

Signature:_____ Date:_____

Before you continue on to the exercises in the following levels have your Journal on standby.

PART THREE

The Twelve Level Course

The Journey of Self Discovery

LEVEL

1

During this level of the course your primary intention is to keep a check on your internal dialogue and silence the voice of doubt. You will learn to discern which 'inner voice' guides your thoughts and drives your actions.

You are encouraged to remain detached and practice becoming an Objective Observer. This will allow you to see yourself, and life, from a much more expansive perspective – bringing you closer to love and greater freedom.

Silencing the Ego's Prattle – Negative Self-Talk

DIVINE TRUTH: Your Point of Power Exists in the Moment.

KEY WORDS: Mindfulness versus Unconsciousness

Being mindful allows you to be an Objective Observer – maintaining your power in the moment, whereas, unconsciousness deters your progress and forfeits your power to implement change.

'Your internal dialogue will indicate just how much care and respect you are willing to uphold in the relationship you have with yourself. Generosity and humility are by far your greatest strengths when it comes to fostering your confidence and trust.'

We all love to surround ourselves with people who offer us praise, encouragement and support. So why is it so difficult for us to do the same for ourselves?

No matter how many worldly possessions we have, or how many accolades we receive, if we are not at peace with ourselves, we will still feel incomplete. The only way we will ever feel whole is by acknowledging the value of our Soul and Spirit.

When we know who we really are we will finally recognize our true worth, whether we stand alone or in a relationship; even if we are stripped of our identity.

So how do we know we are enough? The first and most important step is to master our Ego.

If that sounds like a tall order, consider what you have gone through to get where you are today. Then consider how different your life would have been if you were accompanied by a wise and loving voice that guided you every step of the way – rather than the incessant prattle of your Ego.

As an adult, that responsibility now rests in your hands. You can choose to be extraordinary or remain dissatisfied with yourself. The choice is always yours.

The relationship you have with yourself is the most important relationship you will ever have. It rests at the heart of every other relationship you create. Not just with the people in your life, but with everything in your world.

You are accompanied by your thoughts every second of every waking day. Whenever those thoughts lean towards criticism and uncertainty, you put yourself through unnecessary stress and anxiety, which spring from negative Ego.

To experience more of your True Self stay mindful and conscious of where your thoughts are heading. They ultimately fuel your expectations, which sway your choices – turning the dial on wheel of destiny.

The key is to stay in touch with your feelings. They act as a reliable barometer that indicates the quality of your thoughts. If your thoughts are expansive, they align with love, joy, individuality, and freedom – the course of True North. If you let the self-doubting part of you steer your thoughts, it will lead you up the garden path or drive you into the ground. If you remain sensitive to your feelings, you will know when you have gone off track.

The bottom line is – unless you are compassionate and generous with yourself, and willing to take positive action to support your best interests, your life will remain the same.

Pay particular attention to the areas where you have fallen prey to the belief you are not good enough. Challenge those beliefs – they are simply not true!

Before you make a choice or decision be very clear on where you are coming from. Which part of you is giving direction? Is it the wise and loving caretaker that supports your heart's desires or the 'inner tyrant' – the part of you that plays the role of the Objector/Protector and oppressor?

If your internal dialogue mimics the tone of a strict and critical parent, change your approach – your inner tyrant is wielding its sword. It will cut you down and slash your hopes with the blink of an eye – if you let it.

Remember, every choice and decision you make is based on how you see yourself and who you believe you are. So don't give your Ego the power to assess your status.

Your liberation lies in your power to choose – and that exists in every moment. That's why it is imperative you let go of the past. The labels you give yourself, based on your past experiences, will warrant your expectations in the future. So when your Ego offers you a rundown on your faults, simply pull the plug on its incessant commentary.

Don't argue with it, negotiate with it or attempt to please it – just disengage! Consistently focusing on who you genuinely want to be is the only way you can instigate permanent change. So every time you find you are judging yourself, for whatever reason, stop and practice self-acceptance. No matter who you've been in the past, or what you've done, forgiveness heals all wounds and is crucial for transformation.

When you judge yourself, self-punishment normally follows. As an alternative, offer yourself acknowledgement and encouragement in the same way a loving parent would. All things considered, you are the guardian of your own heart. So every time you feel uneasy or apprehensive, shift your internal dialogue towards acknowledging your gifts and strengths.

This is the simplest way of giving your Soul the attention it is worthy of. Stop and tell yourself that you deserve to be loved in each and every moment, exactly as you are. At the end of the day your happiness depends on the quality of the relationship you have with yourself. So unless you curb self-criticism and consider your true potential, you will continue to disregard your inherent worth.

If you are challenged by negativity it pays to stop and ask yourself this one important question –

'Am I willing to let go of the past and be humble enough to let things be different now?'

Unless your answer to that question is an affirmative YES, you will continue to play chess with your Ego and attempt to seek control, rather than open yourself to being loved.

It is a misconception to believe that you have to compete to achieve results. If you constantly compare yourself to others you will form unrealistic ideas of who you are supposed to be in order to be loved. You will remain susceptible to the belief you are in some way, shape or form – deficient.

This was the case with Jessica, who, despite her long list of impressive assets, was plagued by self-doubt.

She came to see me, nursing a broken heart after struggling with her fiancé's infidelity. Rather than questioning his level of integrity, she blamed herself for his behavior and labeled herself a failure for not being enough. She had fallen prey to the antics of her Ego, seeing herself as inadequate.

Ironically, Jessica was a model whose flawless beauty provided her with a substantial income while also fuelling her obsession to be 'perfect'. Jessica viewed herself under a microscope, magnifying every one of her imperfections. Based on her quiet mannerisms, and the amount of time she spent focused on her appearance, many people she met thought she was pretentious.

Contrary to their opinions, there was very little about Jessica that was superficial. She graduated from university with honors and was actively involved in community service. Trapped by her Ego's condemning prattle, Jessica was merely insecure. She viewed herself as less than, not better than, others, always striving to erase her flaws.

Things slowly began to change when she realized how important it was for her to feel good, rather than look good. It wasn't just her appearance that Jessica was fixated on; she was a perfectionist who strived to be impeccable in most arenas. When I suggested to her that she love and accept herself, she responded in the same way as many of my clients – 'But how?'

I suggested Jessica treat herself with the same respect, care and consideration that she did the people in her life that she loved. She was persistently willing to forgive their shortcomings and accept their weaknesses, offering her generous support and encouragement. Jessica considered that equation and took it to heart. She had been torturing herself far too long and was too tired to continue the struggle.

Rather than give up or give in, she changed the lens through which she viewed life and began to glean the bigger picture. For Jessica, gentleness became the key to her liberation.

Being gentle with herself, in the same way she was with others, allowed her to presence more of her Soul, lifting her into compassion. Jessica's soulful perspective allowed her to see how inconsequential her failings were in the grand scheme of things. She finally realized how hard she had been on herself, and vowed to be more mindful of her thoughts and conscious of her feelings.

Like most of us, Jessica was challenged by negativity on a daily basis. Meditating regularly, she practiced being an Objective Observer – choosing to respond rather than react. When she fell short of her goals or made mistakes, she was far more patient, reminding herself she was still in the process of growing and learning. With every step she took, she was right on track, taming her Ego and discovering more of her True Self.

We always have two choices, we can either pull back, which allows us to be an objective observer, or we can fall asleep under the Ego spell.

If we give our Ego permission to take the driver's seat in our life, we are in for a bumpy ride. Jessica learnt that lesson the hard way. Her broken heart served as the incentive she needed to heal the wounds from her past. It became the catalyst for her to recognize she had initially betrayed herself, by denying the value of her goodness, truth and beauty.

Her self-contempt at times far outweighed her boyfriend's arrogance, which often tested her resilience. He was a man with a penchant for beautiful women, with a wandering eye, who was tempted to stray. Like a child with his hand in the cookie jar, he was eventually caught red-handed with one of Jessica's friends. Despite his declaration of love and loyalty, his Ego successfully sabotaged their relationship, ending their engagement.

As difficult as the pill was to swallow, Jessica was wise enough to see life was offering her an opportunity to grow. She had previously ignored his fickle behavior, turning her attention back to her own imaginary faults.

We all have so many magnificent qualities and yet we can become obsessed with the shape of our thighs, our level of status or the size of our bank accounts. We continue to highlight 'what's missing' and ignore the value of our Soul and the potency of our love. That is the nature of the illusion of this world; it tempts us to forget we are so much more than what we see with our physical eyes.

Our Ego will lie and tell us if we were more we would have more and that if we were better we would be happy. It dangles an elusive carrot that it never delivers. If you start a sentence with, 'if only I had', or 'if only I was' – pay attention! Happiness is not a commodity. Material wealth and physical attributes won't necessarily bring you pleasure. The quality of the relationship you have with yourself will. Success is not just based on how many times you win, or how much you accrue. It is based on how much joy you experience, and how secure you feel in the process.

Although you may not be a model, performer or actor, how often do you feel as though there is an invisible panel or audience reviewing your attributes? Do you have an internal critic constantly sizing you up and evaluating your worth? That critical voice probably shows up in an area where you have experienced disappointment in your past and are still feeling shaky. It takes humility to know things can be different and there is nothing humble about judgment and criticism. Whether it is directed towards us or someone else, it is destructive and hurtful.

When Jessica stopped judging herself and silenced her inner critic, she finally felt free. For the first time since her early childhood, she fully embraced her uniqueness and connected with her Authentic Self.

It takes discipline to stay awake and challenge your negative thoughts. So what is your incentive?

When you carefully monitor your internal dialogue you feel better about yourself. And whenever you feel good about yourself, you feel good about life.

The Voice of Doubt – Your Fears and Failings

As you move toward claiming more of your True Self, keep in mind that self-doubt casts a shadow over your level of self-worth. If your identity becomes more important than your Soul and Spirit, in the same way Jessica's did, you will always feel a sense of being incomplete. At the end of the day, changing your outward persona won't change a thing; unless you also alter the way you view yourself.

If you aren't willing to garner the wisdom from your experiences and leave the past behind, you will simply project more of the same into your future. Until you are willing to adjust your focus, and expand your self-awareness, you will continue to deny the intrinsic power and beauty of your Essence.

As was the case with Jessica, one of the reasons we disregard our true worth is because we have been disappointed, which has left us disheartened. Despite her valiant efforts, there were times that Jessica felt she let herself down because she wasn't able to create or achieve everything she set out to do.

Chances are, at some point in your life, you have faced obstacles where you felt powerless to change your circumstances. During those times, the important thing is to take a quiet moment to sense where you need to stretch your thoughts and review your actions. Don't give your Ego permission to interpret your situation, or orchestrate your response – turn to your intuition; otherwise you won't grow through the experience and your Ego will mar your confidence, leaving you feeling self-conscious or ill at ease.

Sidestepping negative self-talk will help you avoid feeling awkward, which is the key to authentic self-expression. Stepping into the shoes of your Authentic Self will boost your power to attract new opportunities and explore new avenues. Following that path of True North frees you up to enjoy what you do in the world, rather than operating from survival or seeking approval.

Just remember – there is nothing in the outside world that is a hurdle, other than what you create with your own self-doubt and limited perception of who you are and what is possible.

The Voice of Demise –
The Game of Defend and Attack

We are all afraid of judgment and criticism to a certain degree. Feeling exposed or vulnerable, we refuse to express ourselves authentically in fear of being rejected. Like Jessica, we hide the parts of our characters we dislike and wear a mask of pretence. If we wear that mask often enough it becomes a shield we use as a defense.

For Jessica it was important to accept herself fully and then choose who she wanted to be. Otherwise she would continue to hide her insecurities behind a wall of defense, which would have kept away the love she needed to heal and grow.

To shed your armor in a world you believe at times is unsafe can accentuate your fears. However, vulnerability can be a great strength. Most of us are terrified of being vulnerable because we equate it with weakness, which is merely a fabrication of Ego. If you want to receive love and support, it is essential you dismantle your shield and open your heart.

During that process you are obliged to give up control, which is why there are times your Ego resists. Just keep in mind that when you build a defense structure around you, it not only keeps out the things you don't want to experience, it also alienates you from love.

Control and love can never exist in the same space – one extinguishes the other. Interestingly enough, the only reason we vie for control is because on a deeper level, we are afraid of losing the love.

When you are feeling overly vulnerable, the best way to overcome your fears is to remind yourself that love is your greatest ally. If you let your Ego interpret that truth, it will equate love with weaknesses. The way you conquer the Ego is by raising your level of self-worth.

When your Ego keeps score on your status, your self-worth will rise and fall, like a barometer, depending on whom you are with. Seeking outside validation to prove your worth will only leave you susceptible to compromising your integrity. No matter which way you go about it, the only way to break that cycle is to love yourself first. Then you will be more likely to allow others to do the same.

Hiding your true feelings and wearing a mask will only provoke inner turmoil and trigger conflict in the outside world.

Some of us go to great lengths to avoid conflict, others incite it to gain control and get attention. When we feel powerless, we will either push back at the world, attacking others to strengthen our own position or defend ourselves by withholding our feelings and withdrawing. If we feel threatened, we often struggle for control to feel less vulnerable. At which point we simply become self-righteous.

During conflict, the negative Ego has two distinct behaviors in a relationship – defend or attack. You may not use your fists to attack and defend, but a condescending tongue can be just as painful. The antidote to negative Ego behavior is embracing humility and responsibility.

Many a tyrant justifies their behavior by believing they have been victimized, which is specifically how the Ego works. That is why it is important not to blame others or yourself. If you do, you will simply become a victim to your own Ego. You will either dominate the space through overt control or manipulate through weakness – believing you have been hard done by.

Whether you play the persecutor or the victim, you are still operating from a place of fear and domination, which aligns with negative Ego.

At the end of the day, you are the one who needs to be happy when you rest your head on the pillow. No matter where you are in the world, or who you are with, you still have to live with yourself. This is why it is absolutely imperative that you strive to master your Ego. It takes discipline to be mindful – but you are worth every bit of effort it takes.

Charting your course

Write your intention in your journal – where you intend to align your focus.

Because you will be working specifically with negative self-talk, your aim is to disengage from your negative Ego - so write your intention in positive terms.

An example of a positive focus could be:

'During this level of the course, I intend to practice being mindful and refrain from judging myself or others.'

Or you may prefer something more direct like:

'As I progress through this level of the course, my primary focus is to stay receptive to being loved and drop my defenses.'

Choose staements that you are genuinely willing to abide by. Make your declaration of intent in the presence of your Higher Self and Soul, so you know you will make every effort to stand by your word.

Write the following **Pocket Affirmation** *in your Journal and post it in a prominent position as your daily mantra.*

'I am willing to let go of the past and be humble enough to let things be different now.'

Write the Keywords: **Mindfulness versus Unconsciousness**
in your journal and contemplate them on a daily basis. Become consciousness of which of the two you align with more often, to help you assess where you give your power away.

Authentic Self versus Ego – Daily Observations:

As you progress through this level of the course, work through the list of questions below and record the results in your journal. For seven consecutive days make a concerted effort to be conscious of the power of your Negative Ego and monitor your progress. Complete the following chart by answering with either a definative yes, no or sometimes. Pay particular attention to the tone of your internal dialogue – it is an indicator for what is driving you.

When you complete the exercise, look at where you are most susceptible to your Ego's influence. For example you may find that you are not willing to be responsible and your 'knee jerk' response is to blame and deny.

Your point of power exists in the moment – so pay attention! Your aim is to stay awake and not fall asleep under your Ego's spell. Catch yourself and alter your behavior going forward.

How conscious were you today. Did you:

Questions	Day 1	Day 2	Day 3	Day 4	Day 5	Day 6	Day 7
Respond rather than react?							
Communicate authentically rather than defend or attack?							
Acknowledge your uniqueness rather than compare yourself with others?							
Focus on who you are becoming rather than dwell on the past?							
Remain generous with yourself and others rather than being critical and stingy?							
Remain open and receptive rather than push, dominate and manipulate to gain control?							
Remain mindful rather than unconscious?							
Remain responsible rather than blame or deny?							
Remain humble rather than judgmental or righteous?							

Do the meditation for this level for a minimum of 15 minutes at least three times before moving to the next level. You may want to record any insights that arise during that quiet time in your journal.

The process

To master your Ego it is important that you stay humble and practice self-acceptance. Keep in mind that humility has nothing to do with false modesty – it places you in a position of equality, no matter who you stand next to in the world.

If you are generous in the way you view your merits, you will expand the parameters of what you deserve and how much you are willing to receive. Your aim is to change your perception from 'critical judge' to 'loving custodian' – being mindful of the way you view yourself.

Write your answers to the following exercises in your journal.

EXERCISE 1 – PART A:

Pinpointing Your Weaknesses

To discern where you are the most susceptible to self-criticism, make a note in your journal of what you specifically don't like about yourself in each of the following areas:

Appearance – your body and sense of aesthetics

Performance – your ability to produce results and achieve your goals

Contribution – your ability to have impact and make a difference

Creativity – your ability to be imaginative and inventive

Individuality – your ability to value your essence and acknowledge your uniqueness

Love – your ability to love and be loved

Intellect – your ability to think strategically and expand your knowledge

Sensitivity – your ability to be kind, caring and compassionate

Intuition – your ability to be wise, perceptive and intuitive

Pay particular attention to the parts you judge harshly and find difficult to accept. Once you have finished, review your list and pinpoint which area is your 'Achilles Heel'. This is a seemingly small but crucial weakness, which can potentially lead to downfall.

KEY COORDINATE NO. 1

In your journal, respond to the following in the separate section: Map of the Soul

1. My Achilles Heel is _____?

EXERCISE 1 – PART B:

Practicing Self-Acceptance

To shift your point of perception, turn your back on your Inner Critic and open your heart to presence your Soul. Take a few quiet moments to muster your compassion and acknowledge how your self-criticism makes you feel. For the sake of your happiness, are you willing to give up your arrogance and be more generous?

2. What parts of myself am I now pledging to accept _____?

Your Authentic Self as an Objective Observer

Below is a shortlist of attributes that will help you align with your Authentic Self and be an Objective Observer.

Respond rather than react

Communicate authentically rather than defend or attack.

Maintain your sense of worth rather than compromise or overcompensate

Acknowledge your uniqueness rather than compare yourself with others

Focus on who you are becoming rather than dwell on the past

Be generous with yourself and others rather than be critical and stingy

Be open and receptive rather than push, dominate and manipulate to gain control

Be mindful rather than unconscious

Be responsible rather than blame and deny

Be humble rather than judgmental and righteous

Your aim is to become more mindful of where you are coming from and discern which part of you drives your choices and actions.

Where am I coming from and which part of me drives my choices and actions?

_____

EXERCISE 2:

Authentic-Self and Objective Observer – A Day in Review

Review one day within this level and ask yourself – How different would things have been today if I approached life aligned with my Authentic Self?

Start with the statement:

If I was fair and generous – and knew I had everything it takes to succeed – and acknowledged my full potential – this is what I would do differently if I lived today over again _____.

Entering a State of Innocence

Accessing a state of innocence is one of the most important steps you will ever take toward experiencing more love. It aligns with allowance and acceptance, rather than control or resistance. In that receptive state you take a humble attitude toward yourself and the world around you, knowing that life brings continuous change and growth.

Embracing your innocence will help you expand your mind and open your heart. It opens the gateway to your Higher Self and Soul and awakens your intuition.

Practicing this simple technique on an ongoing basis will help you to become mindful and view life from the position of the Objective Observer.

You can do the meditation with your eyes open or closed, in the privacy of your own bedroom or in a quiet spot in nature. Once you are familiar with entering the 'zone' you can practice the technique anywhere. Your aim is to be fully present in the moment and open up to being impressed, rather than generating thoughts or asserting your will.

THE MEDITATION

Sit quietly, take three deep breaths and relax.

Empty your mind of all thoughts and place your Ego aside. With your next deep breath – exhale very slowly and focus on the centre of your being.

Now breathe gently. Become totally receptive, letting go of the past, letting go of the future, still and present in the moment. Say quietly to yourself, 'I know nothing and in not knowing anything, I know everything'.

As you focus on your breathing, sense your connection to your Soul and the essence of All That Is. If any thoughts enter your mind just let them go and continue to expand your awareness.

Your checklist

1. Did you write in your journal on a regular basis to observe your thoughts and feelings?
2. Did you record any Soul-Speak?
3. Have you logged your insights, goals and aspirations?
4. Were you mindful of your intention?
5. Did you take time to contemplate the Divine Truth and the two Key Words?
6. Have you been using your Pocket Affirmation on a regular basis?
7. Have you taken time to meditate for a minimum of 15 minutes on at least three occasions?
8. Have you done your exercises and logged them?
9. Have you been conscious of how your internal dialogue affected you – based on mastering your Ego?
10. If you haven't done any or all of these things then ask yourself – what stopped you?

You may be going into denial or avoidance around the topic for this particular level of self-discovery – what has your Ego been telling you?

Those conversations reflect your limited beliefs about yourself. CHALLENGE THEM! Remember – your heart's desires are at stake.

LEVEL

2

During this level of the course your primary intention will be to uncover and explore your internal self-image, which influences what you attract in life and dictates what is possible.

You are encouraged to take a good honest look at the way you see yourself, beyond your identity, to determine whether your image needs strengthening. Your contemplations will reveal the way you view your potential and expand your self-awareness. They will help you ascertain how you genuinely feel about yourself and identify the 'calling card' you invisibly present to the world.

Seeing Yourself Through the Eyes of Love – Redefining Internal Self-Image

DIVINE TRUTH: You were born with the power to create your own reality and determine the course of your destiny. You either consciously create your reality, or subconsciously allow events to take place in your world.

KEY WORDS: Responsibility versus Blame

You always have two choices in all situations – to accept responsibility as the creator of your reality or forfeit your personal power and blame others for your circumstances.

'Your subconscious communicates through the language of pictures and feelings. That's why it's important you have a strong sense of the qualities you want to develop and a clear vision of the person you wish to become as a reference to build a dream on.'

Over the course of your life, your subconscious has gradually formed an image or an impression of you based on your experiences. That subconscious image mirrors the beliefs you hold about yourself and what you are capable of achieving. It reflects the way you genuinely feel about yourself beyond your logical thoughts.

Your internal self-image may differ in various parts of your life. The way you view your potential in your career may be vastly different than your romantic relationships, friendships and even your recreational pursuits.

Depending on which role you play, and which arena you play in, your confidence levels may alter. The strength of your internal self-image will rest on how much you trust your inner resources and the depth of your character. If your core beliefs are negative in any area, the chances are your self-image is distorted, which lowers your sense of worth. If that happens to be the case, you will dim the light of your Spirit and de-value the essence of your Soul, closing down to love and self-expression.

Your internal self-image affects what you attract and determines what is possible. Therefore, it is absolutely imperative that you stretch your image as you continue to grow. There is often a split between the way a person presents themselves in the world and how they perceive themselves internally. Many people build a strong identity that reflects poise and confidence and yet beneath the surface their hidden insecurities undermine their goals, wishes and aspirations.

Your substance or character is not something that you put on like a coat in the morning and then take off at night. It is something that you live and breathe, a part of your consciousness. No matter what your physical persona reflects, it is how you feel about yourself on a deeper level that fundamentally counts. Your internal self-image is ultimately what determines your fate. Whether you face a promotion in your career, or desire a change in your relationships – unless your image is strong enough to support the experience, it will continue to elude you. Even though you may consciously think you have everything it takes, or logically be the best person for the role, the reality just won't 'stick'. Opportunities may come your way but your feelings are the 'glue' that brings substance to your creation.

For the new job or relationship to land, the subconscious 'impression' you hold of yourself needs to expand to attract and sustain the new experience.

As the custodian that gathers and stores content in your inner world, your subconscious is programmed with vast amounts of information regarding your past experiences. It accumulates and categorizes phenomena and events associating them with specific outcomes.

The best way to understand this principle is to consider the way a computer works. The software holds files of data, which are backed up and stored for future use. Unless the data is reprogrammed, the old files continue to tell a computer what to do and it produces specific results automatically. Your subconscious mind operates in the same way. It holds your beliefs and images and projects them into the world as a subliminal broadcast. People then unconsciously respond to those signals and life delivers precisely what you expect – based on your past experiences.

To change what you see on a computer screen, you need to upload new information and revise the files. Using a similar method, you can reprogram your subconscious. Just keep in mind the language you use is pictures and feelings. The old adage 'a picture is worth a thousand words' portrays the dynamic perfectly. Complex stories can be described with just a single image, which is the way your subconscious receives and transmits data.

When it comes to your subconscious, an image is more influential than a considerable amount of dialogue. Which is why creative visualization is the ideal means to communicate and change your experiences. Through this simple, practical method, large amounts of information can be absorbed by your subconscious in a short amount of time.

Remember – your subconscious knows no difference between your imagination and what you perceive in the physical world.

Your imagination offers you a window into the realm of possibility, a place where dreams are born and inspiration abounds. Who you consistently imagine yourself to be in this world is who you will potentially become. So hold a clear vision of the person you ultimately wish to be to alter your experience.

This was the case with Sarah, who had been stuck in a corporate rut and a marriage that lacked passion and vitality. She finally decided to take a risk and step out of the box. To change her life she not only had to move beyond her fear of facing the unknown, she also needed to see herself as someone completely different.

Sarah surmounted those hurdles by learning to remain focused on the person she ultimately wanted to be, rather than surrendering to self-doubt.

Although that took a certain amount of discipline, the turning point came for Sarah when she was finally willing to acknowledge the value of her dreams.

It takes both courage and commitment to give up a false sense of security and create a brand new life. But with her heart sinking and her health failing, Sarah knew she had to make that choice. Through Body Speak, her food allergies were screaming at her to review what she was willing to digest or tolerate and opt for a more nourishing life.

Although Sarah had no idea what she originally wanted to do, she looked for clues in what her natural talents were and what brought her heart to life. Sarah was a passionate cook with a natural flair for food presentation and inventing recipes. She was a budding talent who had underplayed her culinary skills in favor of a more stable career in financial services.

Coming up with an idea was only half the challenge – she needed to change the way she viewed her potential.

After uncovering her restrictive self-image, she was wise enough to recognize she needed to create her new identity from the inside out. This helped her rebuff other people's negativity and skepticism about her quest to break into the catering industry.

The breakthrough occurred when she was willing to consider the validity of her needs and preferences and not just comply with others. For Sarah that was a first.

Her health and happiness became her number one priority and her emotional energy shifted.

If we refuse to awaken our passion, we sabotage our dreams and dissuade our success. If we continually compromise and are repressed by fear, we are out of integrity with our Soul and out of sync with our authentic self.

The thing that supports us in fulfilling our dreams is the attitude we have about ourselves and the way we feel about ourselves will reflect our summary of life.

Sarah recognized how important it was to follow her heart and give herself permission to grow. While she wrote a business plan and sharpened her cookery skills, she continued to reflect on the depth of her character and slowly developed her inner strength.

For the first time Sarah was carefully crafting a life that inspired her heart, rather than building an identity to seek approval. Consequently her creativity blossomed as she discovered new parts of herself.

Slowly but surely, her identity started to reflect her unique signature and became the perfect vehicle for her to express her specific talents and distinct style. By using her imagination and feelings Sarah started to connect with the qualities of the person she wanted to be. She saw herself as a happy, highly creative person who was an inspiration to others. Embracing that image in her mind provided her with a new level of self-assurance.

In the past, Sarah had subconsciously seen herself as 'invisible'. With her new self-image, she started to perceive herself as 'inspiring'. As a result, her sense of worth increased and her Spirit came to life. Sarah transformed her persona from the inside out and the universe provided her with a platform to celebrate her creativity. As soon as she discarded her old self-image, she attracted new opportunities.

If Sarah had been complacent and continued to tell herself that things would never change, she would still be working in a small office, suffering from chronic fatigue. Instead, she lives a rewarding life as a successful caterer with a husband who is inspired by her passion. In stretching her internal self-image, she finally realized she deserved to be acknowledged, which brought a wave of exuberance into her marriage and attracted a long list of regular clients.

So how did Sarah shift her life from mediocre to magical?

She made it a regular habit to write in her journal and express her thoughts and feelings on a daily basis. She also made notes about her aspirations and acknowledged herself when she achieved her goals.

Each morning, Sarah would sit quietly and connect with her Soul. Even when she was very busy, she would wake up early and take a few moments to become still and centered. Closing her eyes, she would briefly visualize herself with the qualities she wished to embrace, working the field of her dreams. That 20-minute practice became her routine before she got out of bed to face the world. Sarah experienced first hand the power of her imagination and learnt to use it to her best advantage.

Meditation and contemplation are best practiced in the early waking moments, while your subconscious is still receptive. You can then set a positive course for the rest of the day. In the same way Sarah did, if you are challenged by limitations, you can redirect your attention towards the person you wish to become and what you intend to create. This will eventually influence the quality of your choices.

'Who you imagine yourself to be is who you will eventually become. Your internal self-image underpins your creation and holds it in place.'

Your Idealized Self-Image

While creating a vision of the person you choose to become, be careful not to fall into the trap of constructing an idealized image of perfection. During your formative years, particularly your adolescence, you gathered beliefs and formed an image of the person you thought you needed to be to be loved and accepted.

Many of those aspirations are unrealistic – founded on the Ego's ploy and warped conclusions. Attempting to live up to an idealized image gives rise to negative ambitions, which are based on seeking approval. Those aspirations have nothing to do with developing your substance and character. They are merely a means of building a mask to hide your underlying insecurities. Whether that persona requires being curvaceous and sexy, a leather clad biker or a highbrow intellectual, it places conditions on being loved.

Based on our past disappointments, we construct a specific identity to avoid being rejected, abandoned, humiliated or hurt. In the process of maintaining that idealized image, we will often deny our deepest feelings and forfeit our genuine dreams and preferences.

We deny our right to be authentically self-expressed and, as a result, our happiness and the intimacy in our relationships are compromised.

It is important to focus on the essence of the person you want to be, and simply allow your physical attributes to reflect those qualities. As a result, you will become far more confident and much more charismatic.

When you align with your Authentic Self, you are naturally uninhibited and experience greater freedom; rather than being self-conscious and overly concerned about what other people think. This is your greatest clue to determining if you are being swayed by peer pressure, family traditions or the glossy tabloids; or being true to yourself.

The main thing to consider is whether or not you are genuinely holding your best interests at heart. To identify this you have to get in touch with your feelings.

I have spent a lot of time in different parts of the world working as a spiritual counselor. No matter what walk of life my clients came from, or what their aspirations were, I found that most people were far too attached to their identities.

They had a fixed image in their mind of who and what they should be, despite how that made them feel.

It can be very exhausting living up to the unrealistic demands of the

Ego. It will provide us with a never-ending list of what it takes to be 'good enough'. Many of us attempt to impress others, or do the 'right thing' to win their favor. This was the case with Brad who promoted himself as a man of 'affluence and influence'.

With his large house, impressive sports car and a striking girlfriend, Brad stood out in the crowd. But how did Brad feel about himself underneath the regalia?

Although he had a long list of personal assets, he was never genuinely happy and felt incomplete. His fear of being weak continued to haunt him – which drove him to compete. All the while he inwardly saw himself as a 'pretender'.

Rather than acknowledging the value of his Soul and Spirit, he put his material resources on display to attract what he wanted in life. He was like a kid in a sandbox enticing others to come play with his fantastic toys.

Although he was in his forties, Brad was still playing out the lonely, awkward child and his partnerships suffered as a consequence.

Unless we heal our childhood hurts we will project them into our adult relationships to unconsciously seek resolution. There are three places we can operate from in the world – hurt child, wounded adolescent or spiritual adult.

The definition of being a spiritual adult is accepting 100% responsibility as the creator of your reality. At that stage of your development, you also integrate the magic, wonder and innocence of a child, combined with the adventurous nature of the adolescent. You then embrace your authority to choose your destiny based on trusting your resources.

No matter what a person's profession or title suggests, unless they have made peace with the past, and maintain equality in all their relationships, they are still susceptible to feelings of incompleteness.

Brad had a great deal of substance and yet he still didn't fully believe it. He was intellectually brilliant, an extraordinary businessman, a loyal friend, and a loving son. He was inventive, playful, funny and extremely creative. And yet, none of those things were enough to appease him.

Plagued by a distorted internal self-image, he believed that if he lost everything tomorrow, no one would want to be with him. There was one question Brad asked himself over and over: 'Will I ever be good enough to be fully accepted for who I am?'

When that question became too painful, to avoid further humiliation, he projected his inadequacies onto his partners and focused on their faults instead of his own.

To cover up his fractured image, Brad went to great lengths to conceal his insecurity. He had built an unrealistic vision of who he needed to be in order to be accepted and was driven to build an impressive façade to combat his fear of being rejected.

When the woman in his life no longer sang his praises, he turned to someone else to put him on a pedestal. That exalted position was safe for Brad; it helped him avoid intimacy. Rather than being discerning, he was still looking to fulfill his adolescent fantasies, searching for someone or something to rescue him from his hurt.

Brad's behavior patterns continued until he hit the wall during the global economic crisis. After ignoring his Soul's whispers for many years, he was immobilized by Life Speak and his empire came tumbling down.

Although it was initially painful, it showed up as a blessing. It forced him to stop dead in his tracks and turn his attention inward. By claiming more of his sensitivity, Brad started seeing himself in a new light. In a miraculous play of Life Speak, people he barely knew rallied to his aid, showing kindness, generosity and compassion. Humility replaced his arrogance and his relationships took on greater depth and deeper meaning.

In the midst of crisis, Brad finally realized he was genuinely loved.

By practicing forgiveness and self-acceptance, he gathered his inner strength and turned his life around. During the process, he shifted his internal self-image and released his attachment to 'looking good' rather than being authentic. He no longer saw himself as a 'fake' and felt like a man of 'substance'.

Whether or not we can relate to Brad's character, we can all gain wisdom from his story. No matter who we are, or what we do in life, our deepest intention is to experience more love. To do that, we need to let people in, but our tunnel vision and the distorted view we hold of ourselves can prevent us from doing this.

Whenever we allow our identity to become our priority, we override our feelings and deny our True Self. If we base being loved on our persona, rather than the substance of our Soul and the vibrancy of our Spirit, we will compromise our integrity and merely betray ourselves.

After reviewing both Sarah and Brad's stories, you can see it is possible to rise above adversity by claiming more of the power and beauty of your Soul and Spirit.

We are all born whole and complete: claiming that as your greatest truth, you are now ready to begin your journey of self-discovery and uncover more of your True Self. Your aim is to move beyond self-doubt and break your Ego's spell by changing the way you perceive yourself.

Charting your course

Write your intention in your journal. Where do you intend to align your focus?

Because you will be working specifically with self-image, your aim is to shift the way you see and feel about yourself.

Perhaps it is something like:

> **'During this level of the course, I intend to practice self-love and self-acceptance.'**

Or you may prefer something more direct like:

> **'As I progress through this level of the course, my primary focus is to stretch my vision to see myself as a person who is confident and lovable.'**

Choose staements that you are genuinely willing to abide by. Make your declaration in the presence of your Higher Self and Soul, so you will make every effort to stand by your word.

Write this **Pocket Affirmation** *in your journal and post it in a prominent position to refer to as your daily mantra:*

'I am willing to change and be different. I am who I am becoming and not who I have been.'

Write the Key Words Responsibility versus Blame in your journal and contemplate them on a daily basis. Become conscious of which of these two you align with more often, to help you assess where you give your power away.

Do the meditation for this level for a minimum of 15 minutes at least three times before moving to the next level. You may want to record any insights in your journal.

The process

Please remember your internal self-image is the foundation of what you experience in life in every arena, including the relationship you have with your Higher Self and Soul. It is imperative that you learn to use this process as the basis of your work going forward. Therefore it is vitally important that you explore the topic earnestly. Unless you shift the way you see yourself your life won't alter.

Write your answers to the following exercises in your journal.

The first step to pinpointing your true self-image is to look at the quality of your current relationships and the level of your success. The following exercise will help you determine your position by highlighting the areas where you encounter conflict or experience disappointment. It will indicate where you lack conviction and need to strengthen your image.

For your response to be authentic, you will need to get in touch with your feelings. The important thing is to be honest with yourself and let your answers flow.

It is best to write as much as you possibly can to get to the core of the issue. When you rewrite the exercise in your journal, you will need to allow yourself more room than the spaces illustrated in the template provided.

In completing this exercise, remember your internal self-image changes depending on the different roles you play in your life – such as romantic relationships, career, finance, creativity, health and fitness, spirituality, friendships and family. So choose an area where you are the most challenged. You can then repeat the exercise where you need further clarification.

To give you a helping hand with your exercises, there is an example based on Sarah's completed exercises beneath each activity. These are only a guideline – they are not the right answers. The only right answer is one that is right for you.

EXERCISE 4 – PART A:
Defining Your Internal Self-Image

Fill in the blank spaces below to ascertain 'where you have been coming from' in your life in a particular area. Your aim is to see how defended or guarded you are and where you shut down or hold deeper fear or resentment:

1. The area I have chosen to expand is _____.
2. I have been playing out the role of _____ in this part of my life. When I do, I end up feeling _____ and behave in the following way _____.
3. People then respond to me by _____ and I end up feeling _____ and the cycle continues.
4. Select some key words which describe the way this role makes you feel.
5. Choose the one Key Word from above that best sums up your overall feeling when trying to live up to your 'role' and complete this sentence:
I feel and see myself as _____.

Sarah's Completed Exercise:

1. The area I have chosen to expand is my career
2. I have been playing out the role of *powerless and unacknowledged* in this part of my life. When I do, I end up feeling *bored, frustrated, empty and tired* and behave in the following way *I close off to others, withhold my feelings and just get the job done. I have a problem delegating because I don't trust others and so I*

end up doing everything myself. I then get secretly angry and blame people for not offering their support or acknowledging me.

3. People then respond to me by *shutting down and think I am controlling or more than capable of doing everything on my own. They then ignore me or give me even more to do, putting the responsibility back on me and I end up feeling alienated, frustrated, resentful and invisible – like I just don't count* and the cycle continues.

4. Select some key words which describe the way this role makes you feel: *powerless, unacknowledged, empty, alienated and invisible*

5. Choose the one Key Word from above that best sums up your overall feeling when trying to live up to your 'role' and complete this sentence:

I feel and see myself as *invisible*.

KEY COORDINATE NO. 2

In your journal, respond to the following in the separate section: Map of the Soul

What is your negative key word that sums up your overall feelings and image?

Note – if the words you originally write don't resonate strongly enough, find one that really stands out – you can use a title that encapsulates the image. Words such as victim, martyr, loser, fake, failure, flawed, reject, unlovable, hopeless or outsider may be more fitting. Just make sure you choose a word that makes you cringe!

EXERCISE 4 – PART B:

Capturing a Snapshot of your Old Image

Sit quietly and ask your subconscious to bring up a memory of a recent event where you were daunted by negative emotions and challenged by a restrictive self-image. From that specific scenario, choose a single cameo that portrays your image. Hold it clearly in your mind like a single snapshot as you fill in the blank spaces below –

1. My Self-Image is _____.
2. The last time I felt _____ was when _____. I felt _____ because I was _____ . I just wanted to _____. Instead I chose to _____.
3. The Snapshot Image is _____.
4. The Main feeling evoked is _____.

Sarah's Completed Exercise:

1. My Self-Image is *invisible*.
2. The last time I felt *invisible was when I was expecting a promotion at work and they gave the job to someone who was younger and less experienced from outside the company*. I felt *betrayed, angry and hurt* because *I was left feeling powerless. I just wanted to scream and cry*. Instead I chose to *deny my feelings, say nothing. My allergies flared up so I told myself I didn't have the energy to deal with it*.
3. The Snapshot Image is of *me sitting at my desk in front of my computer with red eyes, looking sad and exhausted*.
4. The Main feeling evoked is *hurt*.

KEY COORDINATE NO. 3

In your journal, respond to the following in the separate section: Map of the Soul

Fully describe your negative snapshot image and the main feeling your image evoked.

EXERCISE 5 – PART A:

Building Your New Self-Image

Fill in the blank spaces below to ascertain 'who you consciously choose to become' as the creator of your own reality. This will help to strengthen your internal self-image.

When choosing your new positive key word, here is the main question to ask yourself – If I fully embrace this one specific quality, could I still maintain my old self-image and play out that role? Your answer needs to be – absolutely not!

1. I choose to play out the role of _____ in this part of my life. When I do, I choose to feel _____ and behave in the following way: _____.

2. My expectation is that people will respond to me by _____, which will allow me to feel _____ as I grow into the person I am becoming.

3. Select the positive Key Words in your previous answers – those that stand out which are similar to each other in the way they leave you feeling.

4. Choose the one positive Key Word that sums up the overall feeling and the image it generates and complete this sentence:
   I feel and see myself as _____.

Sarah's Completed Exercise:

1. I choose to play out the role of *powerful, appreciated and inspiring* in this part of my life. When I do, I choose to feel *passionate, fulfilled and energized* and behave in the following way: *I am highly creative and passionate about my work. I operate a successful business, which runs efficiently and attracts well paying clients. I approach life with an optimistic view, knowing I can trust my resources as they grow steadily.*

2. My expectation is that people will respond to me by being *respectful, thoughtful and generous. They value my contribution, appreciate my services and are inspired by my creativity which will allow me to feel unique, happy and valued* as I grow into the person I am becoming.

3. Select the positive Key Words from your previous answer – those that stand out that are similar to each other in the way they leave you feeling.
   Powerful, valued, inspiring, creative, successful

4. Select the one positive Key Word that sums up the overall feeling and the image it generates and complete this sentence:

I feel and see myself as *inspiring*.

KEY COORDINATE NO. 4

In your journal, respond to the following in the separate section: Map of the Soul

What is your one positive key word that sums up your overall feelings and image?

EXERCISE 5 – PART B:

Capturing a Snapshot of your New Image

Sit quietly and let your imagination guide you. Using your positive Key Words from the previous exercise, bring up an image of who you would be, if you embraced those qualities completely. Create a single cameo that portrays the image and feelings you would like to embody. Pay attention to details such as where you are and what you are wearing. Hold a single snapshot clearly in your mind and fill in the blank spaces below.

1. My Self-Image is _____.
2. I see myself as a person who is _____ and I radiate _____.
   I _____ because I am _____. I just want to _____
   and I choose to _____.
3. The Snapshot Image is _____.
4. The Main feeling evoked is _____.

Sarah's Completed Exercise:

1. My Self-Image is *inspiring*.
2. I see myself as a person who is *inspiring* and I radiate *happiness* and *confidence*. I feel *passionate* and *energized* because I am *inspired* and *creative*. I just want to *explore my talents* and *inspire others* and I choose to be *grateful, humble and free to be me while enjoying the things that I love*.
3. The Snapshot Image is *I am standing in a kitchen at a white marble bench, decorating a wedding cake, wearing a crisp white shirt and a black apron with my logo on the pocket. I look happy, healthy and glowing.*

4. The Main feeling evoked is *joy*.

Note – As Sarah grew into her new self-image of 'being an inspiration' – she could no longer play out the role of being invisible or going unnoticed. As a highly successful business owner, she had to be willing to let go of the past and claim more of her True Self.

KEY COORDINATE NO. 5

In your journal, respond to the following in the separate section: Map of the Soul

Describe your positive snapshot image and the main feeling your image evoked?

MEDITATION

Find a comfortable position and begin to relax. Gently close your eyes.

Focus on your breathing and empty your mind of all thoughts. Take three deep breaths and exhale slowly.

Let go of any tension and relax all of your muscles. Become totally receptive, letting go of the past, letting go of the future ... still and peaceful in the moment.

Allow yourself to go into a complete state of innocence. In the back of your mind's eye, bring up the cameo shot of your old distorted self-image. Notice the way you look and feel.

Allow yourself to feel those emotions fully and engage with all of your senses.

Bring up your old key word and see it written in the back of your mind. Feel the emotions associated with it more intensely.

Now exhale gently and release those feelings, as you repeat quietly to yourself, 'I now let go of the past and create myself anew.'

Let the image fade into the background and replace it with the snapshot of your new self-image. Engage with all of your senses and allow yourself to feel those emotions fully.

Bring up your new positive word and see it written in the back of your mind. Feel the emotions associated with it more intensely. Say quietly to yourself, 'I am (*insert your key word*) and am becoming more (*insert your key word*) every day.'

Once you have embraced the image fully and feel uplifted – take a deep breath and gently bring yourself out of the meditation.

Your checklist

1. Did you write in your journal on a regular basis to observe your thoughts and feelings?
2. Did you record any Soul-Speak?
3. Have you logged your insights, goals and aspirations?
4. Were you mindful of your intention on a regular basis?
5. Did you take time to contemplate the Divine Truth and the two Key Words?
6. Have you been using your Pocket Affirmation on a regular basis?
7. Have you taken time to meditate for a minimum of 15 minutes on at least three occasions?
8. Have you done your exercises and logged them?
9. Have you been conscious of how you see and feel about yourself – based on shifting your internal self-image?
10. If you haven't done any or all of these things then ask yourself – what stopped you?

You may be going into denial or avoidance around the topic for this particular level of self-discovery – what has your ego been telling you? Those conversations reflect your limited beliefs about yourself. CHALLENGE THEM! Remember – your heart's desires are at stake.

LEVEL

3

During this level of the course you will explore your fundamental beliefs, which form the foundation of what you manifest in your world. Everything you need to craft the life you have always dreamed of lies within yourself.

You've been using the basic tools of creation every day to generate the world you live in. The essential resources you have artlessly used are your thoughts and feelings – your attitude – your choices and decisions and your beliefs.

The key components that set the creative process in motion are your desire, imagination, and expectation. Your genuine expectations ultimately spring from what lies at the heart of your creation – your fundamental beliefs.

Deciphering the Dark Matrix – Core Beliefs

DIVINE TRUTH: What you create in your physical world is a reflection of your beliefs.

KEY WORDS: Expansion versus Limitation

You have the choice between staying open minded in all situations or limiting your perception. Stretching your thoughts and beliefs will overcome limitation and lead to expansion, shifting the boundaries on your probabilities.

'Every decision you make in your life is based on how you see yourself and who you believe you are. That is why it is imperative you stretch your beliefs.'

The first step to embracing your full potential is to accept the fact that the creative process begins and ends with you.

Although that may be daunting, it offers you complete freedom.

To take that step authentically, you would have to stop blaming outside influences for your mishaps and accept the fact that you attract your own good fortune.

When you make excuses, you deny your power and negate your responsibility. Far too many people equate responsibility with burden, when in truth it offers us freedom. You have the freedom to be who you choose to be and do whatever you choose to do. What could possibly be more liberating!

You are a powerful magnet that attracts your experiences. Every thought has an electro magnetic energy and a belief is simply a thought that is held in your mind. Just as light and sound are a form of energy, a belief can be seen as a pattern of energy.

Each individual pattern or belief attracts certain kinds of events. You have the power to consciously shape your experience by focusing on thoughts and emotions that produce rewarding realities. In order to use your power affectively, you have to be willing to change your beliefs despite your current circumstances. When you change your mental landscape, your outer landscape will reflect your new beliefs.

There are no hurdles other than those you create with your own self-doubt. Any core negative beliefs you have about yourself have little to do with your true potential. They are merely a ghost from your past – a myth carried over from childhood.

Day-by-day you're in the process of growing and changing and, as an adult, you have the authority to formulate your own beliefs and determine what you are capable of achieving.

Although there are many things that have impact on our lives, they do not overshadow one basic rule that governs our world – we all have free will. We all either consciously create our reality, or subconsciously allow events to take place in our world.

If you believe otherwise, you are merely forfeiting your personal power and are susceptible to becoming a victim of circumstances.

The first rung on the ladder to your success is you. So rather than waiting for someone else to endorse your dreams, give yourself permission to have exactly what you want, knowing you have everything it takes to create it.

Your thoughts are always accompanied by feelings. They fuel your imagination, which impresses your subconscious mind to hold and store your beliefs. As the custodian of your inner world, it uses those beliefs as the basis from which to manifest your reality. Therefore you can use images and feelings to plant new seeds in your subconscious mind and alter your beliefs at will.

The more attention you give to a situation the more your subconscious takes notice. That is why it is very important you remain conscious of the tone of your conversations. They stimulate your imagination and feelings, which will communicate your priorities to your subconscious, steering the course of your destiny.

If you continue to shift your thoughts, imagination and feelings toward a desired outcome, rather than dwelling on the past, a new set of instructions impresses your subconscious and your life transforms.

Once you start reprogramming your subconscious with new images, it will test you to see if you are serious about achieving your aspirations. You have to be willing to stand firm and maintain your focus.

Consistency counts: your subconscious is like a very impressionable child that responds to your tuition. Remember, your subconscious knows no difference between the physical world and the world of your dreams and imagination. Therefore, when you continue to visualize your aspirations, seeing yourself differently, you will harness your power to attract new experiences.

For the changes to manifest, you have to sense and absolutely believe that you are ready, willing and able to have what you desire.

You may consciously think you want something in particular, but unless your desire and willingness outweigh your fear and doubt it will remain a fantasy. Until you are willing to challenge your limiting beliefs the things you desire will remain merely a possibility rather than become a probability.

In an hour you have hundreds of thoughts and desires and imaginings, but they don't all manifest. The reality will only actualize in the physical realm if you have a complementary belief that allows the probability to manifest. This is why it is important you remain conscious of what you give attention to and what your underlying intentions are.

Be clear on the thoughts that are motivating your choices and which of your beliefs are driving your actions.

The repetitive thoughts and catch phrases you repeat in your mind are like tape-loops playing over and over again. They become the mantras that reinforce your beliefs. The dialogue that you chant internally weaves a spell that induces patterns of behavior and keeps you chained to the past.

Often your responses in life are so automatic you renounce your self-determination and become compliant. Your choices will either empower or imprison you – along with your limiting beliefs. They are woven through the Dark Matrix of your Soul's Hologram, creating blockages and encumbering your emotions.

Your Dark Matrix contains the vestiges of your past, relating to the times you were hurt, disappointed or felt you didn't deserve to be loved. It is a shield, initially created in your childhood, which was forged by your negative beliefs and fractured self-image. That shield was then compounded in your adolescent years during times of adversity, failure and duress.

This protection, which may seem comforting at times, is in fact a prison that restricts your freedom. It keeps you caught in a continuum of limiting beliefs that deny your spiritual heritage and your divine right to consciously create what you desire at will.

Your beliefs work together in layers or tiers. On the first rung you have your core beliefs, which give rise to a series of associated secondary beliefs. Those secondary beliefs then give birth to a host of interrelated beliefs that form the basis of your reality.

At the heart of them all lie your keystone beliefs, one of which is the linchpin belief that holds all of your other beliefs in place.

It helps to look at the analogy of a tree as an example: The life and image of the tree spring from the seed or kernel. As the seed begins to sprout, it grows roots that hold it in place and a trunk or foundation that develops branches or offshoots. The entire tree emerges from that one tiny seed, which is encoded with a complex pattern of information called DNA. In the same way the tree's DNA generates its lifecycle and image, your core beliefs create a template that forms the base of your creation.

It is your linchpin belief that forms your nucleus. If you extract it, the reality collapses and you dismantle your Dark Matrix. You can then start to awaken more of your sleeping Soul and ascend into the Light Matrix by claiming more of your True Self.

You are in the process of learning to embrace the full scope of your goodness, truth and beauty. That means letting go of the restrictive beliefs you have about who you are and what you are capable of achieving.

It will serve you well to look closely at the limits you have placed on yourself over the years, particularly in the area of what you can and can't have and what you can and can't do. Ask yourself how that makes you feel? Stop and think about that for a moment, because how you feel about yourself and others is what really counts.

We fall asleep under the Ego's spell, ignoring the fact our happiness is at stake. Here is one key point to remember:

Your beliefs create your experiences and your experiences reinforce your beliefs.

You will continue to get caught up in that cycle unless you are willing to sidestep your Ego and consciously reprogram your subconscious mind with new information. That takes love, care and a compassionate heart; which are the only things that can heal the wounds of your past.

'Every human being is worthy or good enough to be loved. Accepting that truth is a choice you make as an individual and your world then reflects your belief.'

It is imperative you remove the restrictive labels, which confine your spirit and close you off from love. Those limited assessments cloud your positive expectations and re-perpetuate old patterns.

This was the case with Robert, who came to see me in desperate need of inspiration.

Although he had been practicing Buddhist meditation for many years, he found it hard to stay peaceful in his turbulent love life. The question he often asked himself was – how do you maintain a state of calm when you are dealing with the people in your world?

The secret is to learn to master our Ego, with its constant negative commentary and judgments. Robert's Ego created far too much separation in his relationships, while he inwardly craved closeness and tenderness.

In his career Robert succeeded in almost everything he undertook but when it came to romantic partnerships, he constantly struggled. I took him through the process of uncovering his distorted internal self-image, which helped him define his limiting beliefs.

Robert was yet another casualty of the escalating divorce rate and was still suffering from the aftershock of a turbulent marriage. When it came to love, Robert had been battered and bruised and needed to soothe his pain.

He had been married for three years - two of which he had spent in emotional torment. His wife had a wicked temper and her cruel tongue had helped to crush his self-esteem.

Robert needed to contemplate life from a higher vantage point before he set off to search for the next 'Miss Wonderful'.

His dreams had been shattered in the past through malice and deceit. To change his experiences, it was essential Robert alter his misconceptions about women and his opinion of how they viewed him. His most destructive belief was that women couldn't be trusted and that loving relationships lead to being used.

Although Robert outwardly appeared to be strong, dynamic and chivalrous, he inwardly felt wounded. In order to prove his merits, he was driven to be a 'hero' to reinstate his worth. His life's story resembled a dramatic parody where he rescued women who eventually betrayed him. When he decided to take positive steps to heal the scars from his past, he created balance in his life by finally being loyal to himself.

As an innocent child, Robert was eager to please and reluctant to hurt others. His mother and father were both highly critical, which weighed heavily on Robert's heart. He was also confronted by their bouts of arguing, followed by long periods of steely silence. Watching their 'war dance' over many years dashed Robert's hopes around equal relationships. His father played out the role of taskmaster, encouraging his son to approach his life like a brave soldier. Robert responded by suppressing his emotions, frightened of being perceived as helpless.

Whenever Robert shared his wins in life, his father would advise him not to rest on his laurels and told him to 'watch his back'. Impressed by his father's comments, Robert grew up subconsciously believing the world was out to get him. His father's favorite motto was 'trust no one'. Consequently, Robert grew up feeling powerless in regard to winning the affections of those he loved.

His parents' legacy influenced Robert to such a degree that he fulfilled the disheartening prophecy that 'love was a battlefield'.

Most of us have a range of guidelines we place on being valuable or lovable. You have to constantly upgrade the quality of your thoughts to successfully alter your beliefs. Until Robert started valuing his feelings, he was constantly motivated by his Ego – his inner critical parent.

Robert was trapped in time, re-running his parents' conversations in his mind. Until he was willing to give up the limited concepts and assumptions he had made about life and love, his romantic partnerships would remain the same.

When Robert finally stopped placing unreasonable demands on himself, he gave up the struggle, relaxed into receptive mode and started practicing self-acceptance. By changing his attitude and modifying his beliefs, he aligned with his Authentic Self and stopped pushing himself to be someone he genuinely didn't want to be. He repeatedly told himself that he deserved to be loved in every moment, exactly as he was. He then turned his focus toward what he wanted to experience and gave up needing to play the rescuer.

To change his situation, Robert rolled up his sleeves to permanently shift his level of entitlement. There were four steps he diligently followed – identify, accept, forgive and transform.

The first step was to identify his self-image and negative beliefs. The second was to accept responsibility as the creator of his reality, and fully own his creation, so the power to change rested with him.

He then needed to progress through the most challenging stage of all – to forgive. Robert had to forgive everyone from his past and most importantly forgive himself. Once Robert made peace with his past, he started to transform.

Setting his sights on romance, he instructed his subconscious by visualizing what he wanted to experience and simultaneously intensified his feelings. This was the way he changed his old self-image and shifted his core beliefs.

This powerful exercise allowed Robert to feel better about himself in the moment, which helped him build his momentum and make healthier choices. He consistently held the vision of the person he aspired to be, which fueled his motivation and sparked his desire.

Robert used this technique until he eventually broke down his old conditioning and created an intimate, loving relationship based on equality.

Strangely enough, the woman he attracted was someone he already knew. When he dropped his invisible shield and became more 'available', Isabelle expressed her interest.

She was bright, independent and very supportive, which shifted his old paradigm around romantic partnerships. Robert was forced to give up his role as the 'wounded rescuer' and create himself anew. From their first official date, to the birth of their first child, Robert knew exactly what a tender, loving relationship felt like.

The level of trust in his relationship with Isabelle served as a clear indication he had successfully shifted his core beliefs. His new self-image of being 'loved' allowed him to feel deeply valued and his life reflected the rewards.

You originally formed your beliefs and therefore you have the power to amend them. Struggling against your past doesn't work. Distinguishing your beliefs and choosing something different is the way you transcend your limitations. Like Robert, you can't eliminate your old beliefs; you simply build a new framework to go beyond them.

In the same way Robert did, you can make peace with your past by forgiving your shortcomings, and declaring you are willing to change. Those simple steps – identify, accept, forgive and transform – bring you in touch with your humility, so you can embrace more of your True Self.

If you are not willing to forgive yourself during the transformation process, you will continue to pay penance. God never punishes us; we punish ourselves. If Robert had not been willing to forgive himself for his mistakes and shortcomings, he would have blocked himself from receiving Isabelle's love. After reflecting on what his old attitude had cost him, Robert realized that was far too high a price to pay.

A Change of Attitude Brings a Change of Heart

By transforming his beliefs, Robert automatically adjusted his attitude, which increased his expectations. Altering the way he approached life allowed him to build a sturdy platform for his future. He turned down the volume on the distrustful part of his mind, which constantly berated his efforts. His focus shifted from magnifying his faults to taking stock of his attributes. Those internal words of encouragement throughout the day helped him develop his inner strength, which in turn boosted his confidence and courage.

Robert also consciously started weaving his new beliefs into the conversations he had with others, grounding them in the physical world. If people made negative remarks about his past relationships or women, he would simply let the comments wash over him, rather than adding fuel to the fire.

If there is anything in your life you wish to alter, it is important you continue to change your point of perception until you no longer follow a negative train of thought. That is the only way any of us can instigate permanent change.

It is a matter of turning your deliberate attention toward what you ideally want to experience rather than setting your sights on what depletes your energy. That doesn't mean you deny your feelings or repress your emotions. You acknowledge them, pinpoint the belief behind them and begin to shift them.

Robert's story demonstrates the point that if you wish to change anything in your life permanently, it is important you uncover your basic beliefs and raise the bar on your expectations. It is also crucial that you are aware of your habitual patterns of behavior and pinpoint the beliefs that they spring from. This will enable you to access more of your personal power and become the conscious creator of your own reality.

Charting your course

Write your intention in your journal. Because you will be working specifically with your beliefs, use a declaration that aligns with shifting your thoughts and attitude.

Perhaps it is something like:

> **'During this level of the course, I intend to challenge my negative expectations and affirm my preferences.'**

Or you may prefer something more direct like any of the following:

> **'As I progress through this level of the course I intend to change my beliefs about never getting what I really want and having to compromise.'**

> **'I intend to be conscious of my thoughts about money.'**

> **'I will watch the quality and tone of my conversations on a regular basis.'**

Choose statements that you are genuinely willing to abide by. Make your declaration of intent in the presence of your Higher Self and Soul, so you know you will make every effort to stand by your word.

Write this **Pocket Affirmation** *in your journal, and post it in a prominent position to refer to as your daily mantra.*

'My point of power is in the moment. I am releasing the past and choose to be free.'

Write the Key Words **Expansion versus Limitation** *in your journal and contemplate them on a daily basis. Become conscious of which of the two you align with more often, to gauge how receptive you are.*

Do the meditation for this level for a minimum of 15 minutes at least three times before moving onto the next level. You may want to record any insights in your journal.

The process

It is important that you remember one crucial point – your thoughts are electromagnetic energy. No matter what occurs in your world, those events manifest because your beliefs form your reality and your life is a reflection of your beliefs. If you believe the world is against you – then it will be. If you believe you have to earn every dollar you make, and money is hard to come by, then your experience will support your belief.

You are not bound to your negative beliefs – you have free will and can use your mind constructively.

It takes time to change your beliefs because the energy of your thoughts needs time to build. Remember, it took some time to form your current beliefs, so it may take a little time before your new beliefs draw the new experience.

When using your affirmations there may be a time when you feel you are being self-deceptive, because your life reflects the opposite of the statement you recite.

If you declare, 'I am successful and surrounded by abundance' and you are still earning a meager salary – your Ego will challenge you. It may tell you that you are dreaming or that you are just fooling yourself. Keep going! Bear in mind that your beliefs also form your self-image, which supports your experience. It is vital that you see your desired outcome in your mind and lift your emotions.

To help you complete the exercises there are example responses from Robert after each activity. Remember these are not the right answers, simply Robert's beliefs and responses; your answers should be unique to you.

Write your answers to the following exercises in your journal.

EXERCISE 6 – PART A:

Defining Your Current Beliefs

Start by reviewing your exercise on self-image from Level 2 and look at the role you played and how people responded. Now view yourself like a character in a movie and ask yourself the following question –

'What would a person have to believe about themselves and the world to create this experience?'

My Old Internal Self Image is _____.

1. I am _____.
2. I have to _____.
3. I always _____.
4. In this area I believe generally that _____.

Whatever title concludes the 'I am' statement will support you in building a belief structure. Those proclamations mold your self-image and help you create an identity in the world and build your character.

Robert's Completed Exercise:

1. I am *weak, scared, useless and gullible, I am unattractive and clumsy, I am a coward, I am boring and unlovable.*
2. I have to *do everything myself, compromise, hide my anger, keep the peace, struggle for what I want, I have to over-compensate, lie about my true feelings and deny my own needs, I have to please women or they will leave, I have to be perfect.*
3. I always *get criticized and end up being rejected, I always feel insecure, I always have to be perfect. I always get used. I always have to suffer, I always feel hurt and alone.*
4. In this area I believe generally that *women are out to get me, not to be trusted, women use men, women are never satisfied, women are cold and selfish – they cheat, lie, manipulate and use men and give little in return, relationships are hard work, marriages don't last, that love hurts.*

EXERCISE 6 – PART B:

Defining Your Current Tier of Beliefs

Remember your beliefs work together in layers or tiers. On the first rung you have your core beliefs, then your secondary beliefs and at the heart of all of them lie your keystone beliefs, one of which is the linchpin belief which holds all of your other beliefs in place.

From your random writing in Exercise 1 – Part A, complete the following statements by choosing the beliefs that really stand out and bring up a strong emotional response.

My Core Beliefs are: I am _____.

Therefore my Secondary Beliefs are: I have to _____ .

Therefore my Keystone Beliefs are: I always _____ .

Therefore my Linchpin Belief is: _____.

Robert's Completed Exercise:

My Core Beliefs are: I am *weak, a coward and unlovable.*

Therefore my Secondary Beliefs are: I have to *over-compensate, lie about my true feelings and deny my own needs.*

Therefore my Keystone Beliefs are: I always *end up being rejected, I always feel hurt and alone.*

Therefore my Linchpin Belief is: *I will never be good enough to have what I want.*

KEY COORDINATE NO. 6

In your journal, respond to the following in the separate section: Map of the Soul

What is your old Linchpin Belief?

Note – Reclaim your power to choose who you want to be and what you want to experience.

EXERCISE 7 – PART A:

Forming New Beliefs

Take a moment to contemplate what you would like to create in your life.

Keeping in mind that your beliefs form the base of your reality, review Exercise 1 – Part A and reverse what you have written. Choose powerful new statements that are the antithesis of those from your past.

Ask yourself:

'What would I have to believe to create what I want?'

Using your notebook, fill in the categories below to clarify your new beliefs.

My New Self Image is _____

1. I now choose to believe _____.
2. My character reflects that I believe I am _____.
3. I constantly tell myself that _____.
4. I expect to be _____.
5. My affirmations are _____.

Robert's Completed Exercise:

My New Self-Image is *loved*.

1. I now choose to believe *I am attractive and confident, I am loved and open. I am trusting; I am strong, creative and perceptive. I am good enough to have what I want, I am supported and valued. I am inspiring and inspired, etc.*
2. My character reflects that I believe I am *loved and cherished. That I consider my own needs and preferences as well as my partner's, I always speak my truth, I always face obstacles with courage, I always communicate and express my feelings rather than swallowing them.*
3. I constantly tell myself that *relationships can be loving and joyful, that women can be loyal and trustworthy, that life offers me everything I need to be happy.*
4. I expect to be *loved and cherished.*
5. My affirmations are: *I can have a relationship with a woman in my life who is gentle and loving, a relationship based on trust, honesty and equality, a partner who has substance and integrity and is tender and compassionate.*

EXERCISE 7 – PART B:
Redefining Your Tier of Beliefs

Keep in mind that your beliefs form the base of your reality.

Review Exercise 6 – Part B and use your notebook to reverse your tier of beliefs. Once again, make sure you use the antithesis of what you had previously written.

My New Self- Image is _____.

My Core Beliefs are _____

Therefore my Secondary Beliefs are _____

Therefore my Keystone Beliefs are _____

Therefore my Linchpin Belief is _____.

Robert's Completed Exercise:

My New Self-Image is *loved*.

1. My Core Beliefs are *I now choose to believe I am loved and appreciated, I am trusting, I am happy and joyful, I am good enough to have what I want, I am supported and valued.*

2. Therefore my Secondary Beliefs are *I choose to have a relationship based on trust, honesty and equality, a partner who has substance and integrity and is tender and compassionate.*

3. Therefore my Keystone Beliefs are *I am loved and cherished, consider my own needs and preferences as well as my partner's, I always face obstacles with courage.*

4. Therefore my Linchpin Belief is *I am good enough to have what I want.*

KEY COORDINATE NO. 7

In your journal, respond to the following in the separate section: Map of the Soul

What is your new Linchpin Belief?

MEDITATION

Find a comfortable position and begin to relax. Gently close your eyes.

Focus on your breathing and empty your mind of all thoughts. Take three deep breaths and exhale slowly.

Become totally receptive, letting go of the past, letting go of the future ... still and peaceful in the moment. Allow yourself to go into a complete state of innocence.

Imagine yourself following a path that winds along the side of a mountain.

Take in the colors of nature as you gradually ascend, enjoying the peace and tranquility as you walk.

Sense your energy building and your confidence growing with every step.

Breathe in the fresh mountain air, allowing it to clear your mind. Your steps become more determined as you walk, you move swiftly and gracefully.

When you reach the top of the mountain, take a moment to be inspired by the incredible magnificence of the vista. The whole world lies before you – your world, waiting to be embraced and enjoyed.

With clarity and conviction, begin the affirmation:

'I now let go of anything that no longer serves me – of worn-out conditions and worn-out ideas. I am whole and complete and therefore my greatest good now comes to pass.'

Let your words be dynamic and powerful as you repeat the statement several times. Hold a sense that the whole universe is listening and eager to respond. Then declare confidently:

'I am _____ (insert your new Linchpin Belief)'.

As you repeat the words, visualize what you intend to achieve and what you are willing to receive. Engage with your senses. Once you have embraced the new belief and feel uplifted – take a deep breath and gently bring yourself out of the meditation.

Your checklist

1. Did you write in your journal on a regular basis to observe your thoughts and feelings?
2. Did you record any Soul-Speak?
3. Have you logged your insights, goals and aspirations?
4. Were you mindful of your intention?
5. Did you take time to contemplate the Divine Truth and the two Key Words?
6. Have you been using your Pocket Affirmation on a regular basis?
7. Have you taken time to meditate for a minimum of 15 minutes on at least three occasions?
8. Have you done your exercises and logged them?
9. Have you been conscious of your beliefs and willing to challenge those that don't support your heart's desires?
10. If you haven't done any or all of these things then ask yourself – what stopped you?

You may be going into denial or avoidance around the topic for this level of self-discovery – what has your ego been telling you? Those conversations reflect your limited beliefs about yourself. CHALLENGE THEM! Remember – your heart's desires are at stake.

LEVEL

4

During this level of the course you will explore your deepest feelings and come to recognize the power and importance of honoring your emotions. You will be encouraged to deal with them honestly and express them appropriately; so you can then move beyond guilt, fear, struggle and control; to experience more joy and freedom.

Harnessing the Power of Resonance – Core Emotions

DIVINE TRUTH: To experience love and freedom, you have to be willing to give up control.

KEY WORDS: Expression versus Repression

Expressing rather than repressing your emotions is an essential key to healthy, authentic relationships. The principle applies not only to the relationships you create with others but also within the relationship you have with yourself.

'All of your feelings are set on one dial. If you refuse to feel specific emotions intensely, you deny yourself the freedom of experiencing all of the others. When you turn down the volume on feelings such as anger and hurt, you will automatically diminish your capacity to feel love, joy and happiness.'

At some point in our lives most of us have complained of being tired, bored or uninspired to varying degrees. During such times we long to feel more love, joy, individuality and freedom. On occasion, we also question why other people can be so insensitive to our feelings. And yet, when we look more closely at the relationship we have with ourselves, how much do we respect our own emotions and respond to them accordingly? Are we willing to feel them fully and express them openly?

In many cases we become impervious to our true feelings and prefer to bury or hide them behind a mask of pretense. We label certain emotions as bad, wrong or even dangerous, fearful of being mocked, hurt, judged or rejected. However, even our negative emotions are there for a good reason: they will show us where our thoughts and imaginings are leading us on our journey of self-discovery. By having the courage to dive deeply into those parts of ourselves, we can become fully empowered and claim more of our True Self.

Your feelings are a precious commodity, worthy of attention. They are your connection to your Soul and the fuel that brings life to your Spirit. Remember, your feelings are set on one dial that determines the intensity of all of your emotions. If you shun emotions such as fear, jealousy or rage, you will simultaneously lessen your enthusiasm and passion.

The meaning you attach to the things that happen in your world is extremely important. What you make things mean will dictate your emotional response. If you give your Ego the power to interpret the significance of certain events, it will trigger a negative reaction. Remember, your negative Ego only ever takes two stands: it will always leave you feeling better than or less than others. Unless you remain centered, you are likely to either shut down or become defensive. This is why your negative Ego is an adversary on your path toward unity and oneness, it inhibits your receptiveness to being fully loved, creating areas of separation.

The things that obstruct your way are your blocked emotions, stifled creativity and limiting beliefs. They hang there suspended, distorting your view of the world and how much of your potential you perceive.

Whenever you fully embrace one feeling or emotion, you enter into that 'state of being'.

On an essence level, your feelings, whether you label them 'good' or 'bad' are from the same source; they simply vibrate at different frequencies. Each state of being emits a particular resonance or energy field. As an example, compassion, gratitude or joy have a different vibration or feeling than loneliness, envy and blame. The higher octave states of being align with love. As the frequency of each emotional state lowers, it gravitates towards fear, descending to the lowest point, which is hopelessness and despair. At this point your negative Ego has full control.

The higher states of being are expansive and the lower states are constrictive. When you align our awareness with a particular emotional state, you will attract things in your world to support the experience. Gratitude begets more to be grateful for. Blame promotes blame. Anger attracts situations that activate further anger and love invites love.

It is important that you honor our feelings and learn to use the power of their resonance to transform your reality. It takes practice to learn to shift gracefully from one state of being into another. If you are able to alter your resonance and transform your state of being at will, you will remain centered and operate in the world from a place of confidence, aligned with your Authentic Self.

Through your internal senses and imagination you can flow from one state of being to the next, depending on how willing you are to give up our control. The more you learn to trust your feelings, the more you will acknowledge your inherent power and express yourself authentically in the world.

Diverting your attention from particular emotions in hope that they disappear will only push them into the unconscious. If you continually deny them, they will eventually pop up to be dealt with through Soul-Speak.

Your Soul will always give you an indication of where you are out of balance. If the masculine side of your nature suppresses the feminine, or your mind overrides your feelings, you will risk becoming numb or, worse still, experience physical ailments or Body Speak, which is a final desperate 'shout' from your Soul that something isn't right. This was the compounding problem my client Georgia was forced to face with her escalating body weight.

When Georgia first came to see me she was tipping 100 kilos on the scales. As the CEO of a thriving company, she believed it wasn't safe to be overtly sensitive, especially as a female. Consequently she was carrying a hefty load of stuck emotional debris that placed an enormous amount of pressure on her heart – both literally and symbolically.

Georgia wasn't willing to trust her feelings, and expressing too much emotion was strictly taboo. She relied heavily on the assertive side of her nature to get what she wanted in life, priding herself on her sharp intellect. If her fears surfaced, she would push herself harder to gain control and reach for food as source of comfort. When Georgia overindulged, it left her feeling 'comfortably numb'. Food and work became an anesthetic for her underlying distress. She overindulged in chocolates, rich desserts and sweets to compensate for her loneliness. What Georgia really craved was intimacy, closeness and tenderness. Yet the irony was she was terrified of being vulnerable.

Even though Georgia was a wife, a corporate executive and an intelligent adult, for most of her life she had been operating as a child - unwilling to be fully responsible for her own wellbeing. She felt very isolated even though she had a husband, countless friends and a very large staff. By creating a shield of defense, she had continued to detach on an emotional level, gradually drawing away from others. Closing down left her feeling lonely, no matter who she was with.

Georgia had always been the primary breadwinner in her relationship with Adam. She secretly wanted someone else to take care of her but was terrified of trusting her husband to that degree, fearing she would become powerless. By choosing a partner who lacked ambition and drive, she had complete control, maintaining her independence by calling most of the shots.

Adam was an unassuming man who was gentle and highly creative, preferring to work at home in his small design studio rather than enter the corporate arena. He was a talented artist who enjoyed illustrating children's books, earning a reasonable, steady income. He loved to cook and was somewhat of a wine buff, preparing dinner for Georgia most nights of the week. When Georgia arrived home tired and grumpy, he would offer her a sympathetic ear and refrain from making too many comments.

Georgia didn't take kindly to criticism and so Adam was always conscious of saying 'the right thing'. In the same way that Georgia was squelching her emotions, Adam denied the intensity of his feelings. He withdrew emotionally and withheld his opinions to avoid hurting her or being shot down. This cycle continued until Adam became concerned about Georgia's health and their potential to start a family.

Although Georgia loved Adam, there were times she covertly resented him for having such 'an easy life'. Rather than expressing her discontent, she hid her emotions, fearful of losing him, burying her deeper sense of not deserving. Her denied rage doused her joy, passion and spontaneity and as a result she suffered from insomnia and anxiety attacks.

Rage is not merely expressed as intense anger; it can also emerge as shame, depression and a resistance to being loved, which were all of Georgia's symptoms. Unless she was willing to trust herself and Adam enough to get in touch with her feelings, and voice them openly, she would remain trapped. As a result, their relationship would simply stagnate and suffer.

Fortunately, when Georgia started processing her emotions Adam agreed to follow suit. Although he usually avoided conflict, and preferred denying his hurt, anger and fears, he knew things needed to change. Unless two people in a relationship grow together, they will eventually grow apart. Adam was wise enough to see that unless he opened up, he would continue to give his power away.

As a result, they promised to be honest with one another and talk things out, creating a safe space in their relationship. That was the first step. The second was to take action by diving into the heart of the issue and facing their fears.

Even though Adam was there to offer Georgia love and support, his contribution would have remained impotent until she was willing to respond by honoring her emotions and deepening her relationship with herself. Although it was unfamiliar territory for Georgia, she turned her attention inward, using journaling as her primary means of getting in touch with her feelings. The more Georgia embraced her feelings the more she could see she had constructed a self-imposed prison, which separated her from being fully loved.

She realized how much she had tortured herself over the years and how she had kept people at arm's length. Not only to protect her from being hurt, but also to protect others from her denied rage. There was no jailer holding her captive other than her negative Ego and the voice of her own Inner Tyrant.

Just like Georgia, we all need to face the 'Objector/Protector' and the Inner Tyrant and learn how to accept, rather than fear, the intensity of our emotions. We can interact with others and yet, because of our fears, there is a part of us that wants to stay separate. We can easily find ourselves going through the motions in a relationship and no longer 'feel' related. This is a sure sign we have put up our defenses and detached from the core of our feelings.

Yet beyond our fears we long to be completely acknowledged and loved. Life lacks luster when we look at the world through shaded eyes. We can't feel the warmth of the sun on our face if we are carrying an umbrella to protect us from its rays. If we block our feelings or distrust them like Georgia did, no matter what we create, we simply won't enjoy the benefits.

You need to experience the depth and the intensity of your emotions to fully release them. If we look at our emotions like a pool of water, some of us are afraid to dive into that pool, floating on the surface or wading in the shallow end.

So why are we afraid to feel?

Often we fear drowning in our emotions or 'getting in too deep'. We are afraid of the intensity of our emotions for fear that we will lose control or be seen as too emotional.

We may be concerned that we will get lost or 'go off the deep end' if we 'give in to' our emotions; but feeling our emotions and honestly and genuinely expressing them stops us from doing just that. People who do go over the edge do so because they have suppressed their emotions to such a degree that they come pouring out – sometimes as destructive or violent outbursts. Our thoughts and feelings need to be processed or the pressure builds up.

We can also be afraid that expressing our emotions means that emotions run our life – yet they already do. Our emotions motivate the games we play, including our need to manipulate and try to control others and what happens in our world. It is our emotions and not our thoughts that ultimately drive us. Yet, behind our feelings lie our core beliefs, which is why we often unknowingly operate from hurt child or wounded adolescent.

There may also be a fear that our life may change if we move beyond our comfort zone. We crave more out of life and yet we are unwilling to let go of what no longer serves us, for fear of having nothing. This is a no-win situation because we block ourselves from having our heart's desires.

Although we may be afraid of losing a relationship, we need to be clear that by holding on to something that does not make us happy, we are forfeiting our personal integrity. If that is the case, we need to consider the fact that when we resist change we deny our true worth and impede our potential to grow.

We may also refuse to express our emotions in order to 'keep the peace'. The irony is, we will end up feeling inner unrest and jeopardize our own happiness anyway. Once we honor our emotions, and honestly and genuinely feel the depth of them, we change. The things we used to put up with in life are no longer acceptable. Shifting out of a rut or old habits awakens our desire and we begin to explore new possibilities.

The best way of dealing with your emotions is to acknowledge them. Feel them with intensity and depth and express or vent them in a safe environment, in an appropriate way.

One of the most effective ways is to write out your feelings. This is one of the reasons using a journal is so valuable. Pour your emotions out onto the page until you are fully spent. Don't edit or judge the information – just get it out. You may feel more secure using sheets of paper you can destroy when you are finished.

Writing a letter to someone you have unresolved issues with is also a powerful way to express your feelings. This works particularly well if you are angry, as long as you burn the letter and don't send it! If you still need to communicate with the person face-to-face, vent the intensity of your emotions first by releasing most of the emotional charge privately.

If you are dealing with rage, you may even want to beat a few pillows or do a few rounds of boxing with a punching bag at the gym. Don't swallow that emotion – get it out!

Another way is to go into a meditation and imagine yourself having a conversation with a person you need to communicate with. Give yourself permission to rant and rave if you need to or have a good cry. Keep going until there is nothing more to say.

As an alternative, you may want to call on a trusted friend or family member and ask them if you have permission to vent in their company with no holds barred. If they are wiling to act as a sounding board and just listen, rather than judging or assessing your circumstances, this can be a favorable option. Make certain they can remain detached enough to respond supportively and not react. Venting can allow you to put your emotions into perspective so you can choose a positive course of action to create change.

The steps to remember are – identify the emotions – feel them intensely – express them – resolve them – and release them.

Once you have processed your thoughts and feelings, you can then reprogram your subconscious mind with new images and feelings that support your wellbeing. If you allow yourself to wallow in your negative emotions for too long, without completing this entire process, you will remain stuck.

Charting your course

Write your intention in your journal. Where do you intend to align your focus?

Because you will be working specifically with your emotions perhaps something like:

> **'During this level of the course I intend to indentify my emotions, feel them intensely and express them fully.'**

Or you may prefer something more direct like :

> **'As I progress through this level of the course I will continue to shift my emotional resonance and aim to be happy.'**

Choose statements that you are genuinely willing to abide by. Make your declaration of intent in the presence of your Higher Self and Soul, so you know you will make every effort to stand by your word.

Write this **Pocket Affirmation** *in your journal and post it in a prominent position to refer to as your daily mantra.*

> **'I am and becoming happy, joyful and free. I honor my heart and express myself authentically.'**

Write the Key Words **Expression versus Repression** *in your journal and contemplate them on a daily basis. Become conscious of which of the two you align with more often, to help you assess where you give your power away.*

Do the meditation for this level for a minimum of 15 minutes at least three times before moving onto the next level. You may want to record any insights in your journal.

The process

During this level of the course, your main focus will be to monitor your feelings and lift your emotional resonance. Below is a chart you can use to help you identify your emotions and see if you are in an expansive state.

Each state of being carries a different vibration that has a magnetic pull. When you align your awareness with a particular emotional state, you will attract things in your world to support the experience. It is essential that you learn to ride those waves and steer your emotions, rather than resisting or repressing them. By avoiding pain, you will also close down to pleasure and steer further away from love.

The higher states of being are expansive and the lower states are constrictive. If you are willing to dive deeply in the pool of your emotions you will begin to create a field of force – you will create a new resonance that will lift you into a different reality.

Scale of emotional frequencies – Emotional Scale Chart

LOVE/JOY/INDIVIDUALITY/FREEDOM

HAPPINESS/PASSION/COMPASSION

ENTHUSIAM/EXCITEMENT/ALIVENESS

GRATITUDE/HUMILITY HOPE

OPTIMISM/CURIOUSITY/CONFIDENCE

TRUST/CONTENTMENT/SATISFACTION

CONFUSION/DOUBT/WORRY

OVERWHELM/DISAPPOINTMENT/PESSIMISM

PITY/SADNESS/GUILT

ANGER/BLAME/RESENTMENT

FEAR/ANXIETY/TREPIDATION

HURT/SHAME/VICTIMIZATION

ENVY/JEALOUSY/RAGE

LONELINESS/EMPTINESS/WORTHLESSNESS

HOPELESSNESS/GRIEF/DESPAIR

When you recognize that you take on a particular emotional state frequently, you can break the habit by consciously shifting your resonance. As an example, if you find you often experience depression or sadness, your option is to access a state of joy. To jump from sadness to joy in one fast leap may be a challenge. It is easier to start shifting by accessing another quality that acts as a stepping-stone to the higher state.

Perhaps you could start by moving up the scale from a state of sadness, into worry, to trust, to gratitude, to happiness and then into a state of joy. This would involve engaging fully with your feelings, expressing, resolving and releasing as you go. Get clear on your underlying beliefs and use your imagination to focus on your preferences. Your aim is to create a new field of energy and shift your resonance so you alter your reality.

EXERCISE 8:

Identifying, Expressing and Releasing Your Emotions

Over the course of the next few days, stay in touch with your feelings to get a sense of which three emotions you naturally gravitate towards. On a daily basis use your journal to process your emotions so you get into the habit of expressing yourself authentically.

The steps to remember are: identity the emotions – feel them intensely – express them – resolve them – and release them. Once you have processed your thoughts and feelings, you can then reprogram your subconscious mind with new images and feelings that support your wellbeing.

Questions To Ask Yourself:

Identify: *To identify your emotions, just ask yourself : 'How does this situation make me feel?' Then ask yourself: 'How do I feel beneath that'.*

Keep asking that same question until you get to the root emotion.

Feel: *Once you pinpoint the root emotion, feel it as intensely as you can. Allow yourself to sit in that state of being, fully submersed in the energy. Don't resist – just be with it.*

Express: *Give yourself permission to express the emotion by writing about your complaint in your journal. Write what thoughts come to you and don't edit. Just vent until you feel your energy settle.*

Resolve: *Assess the current meaning you have attached to your circumstances and define your underlying beliefs. Now search for deeper meaning and understanding by defining what you can learn from the situation.*

Make a note in your journal of where you need to shift your attitude and alter your beliefs.

Release: *Give up your desire to control and move into a state of innocence. Be humble enough to let go of the past, knowing things can be different.*

Lift: *Use your imagination to evoke new images and allow your feelings to respond. Align your thoughts and attitude with your preferences until you shift your resonance.*

Expand: *To fully ground your experience, take positive action. By planting seeds for your future when you feel optimistic, they will take a firm root. That old expression 'make hay while the sun shines' is one that applies here. So no matter how small, take at least one small step towards creating your heart's desires. It can be as simple as declaring your intentions outwardly to a friend, or making a phone call to enroll in a course: do something to follow through physically.*

In your journal, respond to the following in the separate section: Map of the Soul

Make a note of which three emotions you naturally gravitate towards.

Notes on Georgia's Completed Process:

When Georgia got to her root emotion, it was anger. Guilt was the emotion she used as a distraction to get to the truth. It was a feeling she was much more comfortable with and it was usually accompanied by sadness.

What lies beneath guilt is an anger that we believe we don't have a right to feel. Because Adam was so caring and supportive, Georgia felt guilty about always being grumpy and she was sad that things couldn't be different. On a deeper, more honest level, she was genuinely angry. Those fine layers of anger had slowly built up over the years, resulting in depression. Depression is often denied anger so by refusing to feel and express the full intensity of her anger, Georgia shut down, becoming rigid.

Once she expressed her anger and hurt, by writing a series of letters to her estranged stepfather, she became much more vibrant and started to lift. Part of her process was to garner the wisdom she gained from their tempestuous relationship and then burn the letters. She realized that being subjected to his strict and callous behavior, she learnt to be resourceful, independent and incredibly strategic. As a successful entrepreneur, they were some of her strongest assets.

By acknowledging those qualities and being proud of her achievements, she could take back the power she had once given to him. By releasing her resentment, which chained her to the past, she tempered her stride and became more receptive.

After burying the ashes from her letters in her garden, she completed the ritual by planting a small orange tree in the same vicinity. For her this was a sign of letting go of the past and celebrating new life. She took a few quiet moments every morning to water the soil with love and gratitude, knowing she had claimed her freedom.

EXERCISE 9:
Shifting Your Emotional Resonance

Honoring our emotions, while we remain sensitive to the feelings of others, is one of the most significant lessons we will ever learn. Although it poses a challenge, it is a crucial step to maintaining our personal power and upholding harmony in our relationships.

To genuinely bond with someone, regardless of the type of relationship, we need to match their emotional resonance. If one person is happy and the other is sad, they can communicate with words but won't fully connect unless their feelings are parallel. In order for them to engage, one would have to move up or down the scale of emotions to meet the other. The rule of thumb is not to move down but to hold the space for the other person to move up, assisting this transition through remaining non-judgmental.

No one can drain your energy unless you allow them to. You are responsible for your own feelings in the same way that others are responsible for theirs. Although we have impact on each other, we can't make anyone feel anything. We each choose the way we respond or react. However, we still need to be mindful of the effect we have on others if we are committed to being a spiritual adult.

The Art of Being Fully Present

This exercise will help you get into the habit of consciously choosing your state of being – no matter who you are with. The main thing is to not get hooked by negative Ego – yours or anyone else's. Don't deny your emotions, just disengage from negativity and lift! Your happiness is important – claim it and maintain it.

Daily Observations: *Over the course of the next few days, monitor your feelings and practice maintaining your emotional resonance. Stay mindful and be very clear on the meaning you attach to situations and watch your negative expectations. Be humble enough to know people and things can change and be different. At the end of the day, make a note in your journal of where you got hooked and why.*

Your Trigger and New Choices: *Record which specific emotion stands out that triggers your descent into the lower vibrations. It may be frustration, doubt or pessimism or perhaps sadness, anger or hurt. Your aim is to pinpoint the trigger and consciously choose to go up rather than descend, whenever you feel that emotion. Choose a more expansive state, such as wellbeing, optimism or happiness and lift your resonance. You can do this by honoring your feelings and shifting your point of perception.*

In this context, the definition of the word honor is to be honest, fair and show integrity in your beliefs and actions. This will bring you in touch with your Authentic Self and align you with expressing your highest truth.

KEY COORDINATE NO. 9

In your journal, write the response to the following in the separate section: Map of the Soul

Record which emotions trigger your descent.

KEY COORDINATE NO. 10

In your journal, respond to the following in the separate section: Map of the Soul

Record which of the emotions or states of being you choose to aim for.

Notes on Georgia and Adam's Process:

Based on outward appearances, Adam and Georgia were a happy, harmonious couple. Yet beneath the surface they were emotionally estranged. Behind closed doors, Georgia was often impatient frustrated, sad or angry – covered by a veil of guilt. Adam fluctuated from being optimistic to doubtful and then slid into fear and hurt. For Georgia and Adam to fully engage emotionally, one person would either have to lift their resonance or descend to meet on common ground.

As a couple, they got into the habit of monitoring their own feelings and watching where they forfeited their power in their partnership.

As a result, they became far more responsible for their own feelings rather slipping into blame, righteousness or victimhood. Whenever they started to descend, they practiced shifting toward compassion, stretching to find deeper meaning and understanding in their relationship. By lifting into compassion they experienced a stronger sense of connectedness, rebuilding their trust. Being far more considerate and tender with one another, they eventually lifted into a state of happiness. Georgia became much more playful with Adam, which allowed her to rekindle the romance in their marriage and express more of her love.

MEDITATION

Before you begin your meditation look at a particular situation you are currently facing, or at an issue from your past, where you are still dealing with unresolved emotions. If you are not happy with the way you dealt with the situation, you can learn from the experience by playing it out in a meditation and altering your response.

Make sure you feel your emotions fully and express them openly from a place of power, humility and autonomy. Your aim is to honor your own feelings while you remain sensitive to the feelings of others. Just make sure you don't compromise your integrity or repress your emotions. By practicing in meditation, you will be well prepared if you face a similar situation in the future. It will also lay a new track or program in your subconscious mind.

හ

Sit quietly, close your eyes, take three deep breaths and relax.

Empty your mind of all thoughts and place your Ego aside. With your next deep breath – exhale very slowly and focus on the centre of your being.

Start to review a particular area where you feel unsettled. Let the images come to you and allow your inner-senses to respond. Rather than analyzing the situation, become aware of your emotions and express them appropriately by honestly and openly communicating your feelings.

See yourself altering the situation by responding from a state of autonomy – knowing your intrinsic worth. Allow yourself to be in touch with the core of your feelings, rather than surface emotions.

Visualize your desired outcome and connect with the energy of your Authentic Self. During the process, remain humble, give up control and allow yourself to be lifted into an expansive state.

Once you feel a sense of completion, gently bring yourself out of the meditation by slowly opening your eyes and take a few deep breaths.

Your checklist

1. Did you write in your journal on a regular basis to observe your thoughts and   feelings?
2. Did you record any Soul-Speak?
3. Have you logged your insights, goals and aspirations?
4. Were you mindful of your intention?
5. Did you take time to contemplate the Divine Truth and the two Key Words?
6. Have you been using your **Pocket Affirmation** on a regular basis?
7. Have you taken time to meditate for a minimum of 15 minutes on at least three occasions?
8. Have you done your exercises and logged them?
9. Have you been conscious of honoring and expressing your emotions?
10. If you haven't done any or all of these things then ask – what stopped you?

You may be going into denial or avoidance around the topic for this particular level of self-discovery – what has your Ego been telling you? Those conversations reflect your limited beliefs about yourself. CHALLENGE THEM! Remember – your heart's desires are at stake.

LEVEL
5

During this level of the course you will decipher the silent contracts you abide by in your relationships, which set the parameters of your self-expression and how much you are willing to receive. These agreements, established in your childhood and adolescence, give rise to the 'life-scripts' you play out on a daily basis. Those psychic contracts remain in place until you formally end them. Your aim will be to break the contracts and rewrite your decrees, so you are free to reclaim more of your True Self and chart a new course for the future.

Uncovering your Silent Contracts – Negative Scripts

DIVINE TRUTH: You have free will.

KEY WORDS: Autonomy versus Conformity

Being autonomous or self-ruling is an important part of accepting responsibility as the creator of your reality. Conforming to the criterion set by the general consensus will leave you susceptible to forfeiting your freedom of choice and giving your power away. Autonomy versus conformity also supports you in honoring your preferences and being authentically self-expressed.

'We write the script and choose our destiny; the universe simply provides the materials and fills in the blank spaces.'

Beyond the cordons of our day-to-day activities, we communicate with one another on a subliminal level through the unspoken word. This subtle transmission is conveyed from one subconscious mind to another, like a 'psychic telephone network'. Energetically, we are all part of the unified field. There are invisible threads or streams of consciousness that intrinsically connect each of us. We individually send out messages through the ethers, encoded with the details of our life-scripts. Those programs encompass our hidden agendas, which we are bound to live out. People unknowingly respond to our scripts by playing out a complementary role, fulfilling our forecasts. They appear as players on the stage of our life, complying with unspoken agreements, or psychic contracts, many of which uphold negative behavior patterns.

Just as a scriptwriter drafts a story and creates certain characters, you also orchestrate the events in your life and choose the outcome. In the same way an actor recites his lines on cue, your habitual dialogue emerges from a tale that hangs in the ethers. You bring credence to your performance by throwing yourself into the part, delivering your lines with 'meaning'. From a metaphysical standpoint, your feelings bring substance to the illusion of the physical world and what you 'make matter' will eventually take on form.

Good actors immerse themselves in a part to such a degree that they lose site of their true identity. Their performance becomes so believable that the audience is temporarily entranced, believing this to be their true identity. It is the same for each of us; we give so much credence to the roles we take on in life and the scripts we play out, we make our identity far too real. We become entrapped by our fixed agendas.

Where your attention goes your energy follows; the things you consistently imagine to be true shape your expectations. It is your underlying 'intention', or agenda, combined with where you place your 'attention', which determines what you attract. Using the key principles of 'intention and attention', you can entirely shift your reality. The trick is to stay awake and consider who you ultimately want to be and not follow a standard set of cue cards.

By building your strength of character, you can amend your story and change the way you automatically respond to what shows up in your world. The first step is realizing that you are the writer, producer and director with the power to dictate the outcome in all of your endeavors. There is no puppet master behind the scenes, pulling the strings to orchestrate your movements. You have free will.

When we were young children, our primary intention was to love and be loved while we followed a path of self-discovery. Navigating our way through a variety or interactions and experiences, we slowly developed our strengths and explored our talents. On occasion that journey was turbulent, which triggered uncertainty, fear and hurt. Still feeling unsure of ourselves, while building our sense of personal trust, we searched for something or someone in the world to act as a safeguard. If our concerns were not effectively addressed they intensified, eventually becoming stumbling blocks.

During your formative years you viewed your parents or guardians as a vital source of love and protection in your world. They provided you with your primary mainstay, which at times left you feeling vulnerable. Needing to be secure, you assessed which of their qualities and customs would bring you reward and rejected the parts of their nature that caused you unrest. You either mimicked their behavior or rebelled against their influence, determining what worked for you in regard to getting what you wanted in life and also being safe. There were times you were told you were bad or wrong by your guardians, teachers or peers, at which point you assumed you weren't good enough.

These sources of learning were not necessarily ill intentioned. Much of what they taught was part of their own conditioning and what they believed would protect you from a world they didn't trust or fully comprehend. Sometimes, they were harsh, callous or mean. Out of anger, possessiveness, jealousy or fear, you were controlled or punished. During that process, you placed restrictions on yourself that confined you to a world of limitation. In truth, you can be anyone, have anything and do anything you choose to, with harm to none. Yet, although your parents may have encouraged you to be all that you could be, there were probably sacrifices and conditions attached to that agenda.

Based on your fear, shame and self-doubt, you agreed to behave in a certain way in order to avoid being abandoned, humiliated, betrayed or rejected. They are the silent contracts you firmly adhered to, to prevent you from being hurt. Those psychic contracts include blanket statements such as, 'I will be exactly like my mother' or 'I will never be like my mother' or 'I will live your dream not mine' or 'I will not be any more than you expect me to be.'

The contracts become binding and produce the scripts you live by. You then play out a role such as – the unrequited lover, the noble martyr, the struggling artist, the peacemaker, the knight in shining armor or another character that fits one of the mythical archetypes.

Each clause in the contract states a decree of who you consented to be. That invisible treaty contains sub-clauses that forfeit your rights and deny your potential. They proclaim what you will and won't express, setting the conditions for your relationships.

Those key declarations of intent gave birth to your negative scripts, which reflect your core beliefs. Part of your ultimate destiny is to break free of those contracts as a spiritual adult, so you can finally become autonomous. Spiritual sovereignty involves taking your power back from everyone you have ever given it to and retrieving the lost or denied parts of yourself. Your psychic contacts have helped to define you, diminishing the full capacity of your Soul and Spirit.

'You have to be willing to leave the past behind, in order to create new experiences. Otherwise you'll project your insecurities into your future relationships, and continue to attract more of the same.'

Your Defining Moments

The small cameos you hold in your memory will often point to the defining moments in your life, which have left an indelible imprint on your heart and mind. Those memories offer you clues to what you believe is important in life and bookmark the experiences that have built your character. They serve as signposts to where you have either claimed or denied more of your strengths, power and worth.

Whether they evoke positive or negative responses, they stand out as the destiny points on the Map of your Soul. Amongst those experiences were those that triggered an intense emotional response such as fear, hurt and loneliness. These are the defining moments where your survival mechanisms were put in place.

During such times your psychic contracts became more exaggerated and firm decrees were laid down. You made pledges that you would or wouldn't be a certain way – ever again. Those definitive statements were then reinforced by your feelings and imaginings. Every cell of your body stores memory, in the form of coded electrical impulses, which create an electromagnetic field. The information stored in that memory creates a template in the Dark Matrix, which holds a web of intricate behavior patterns that diminish your light or aliveness.

The blueprints of your psychic contracts remain in your field until you clear them. The prominent statements that stand out in those agreements will reveal the laws you instinctively abide by on a daily basis. To avoid the consequences of breaking those laws, you buried them in your unconscious mind and continue to live into them. You will be free of their hold when you uncover, decipher and negate them, reclaiming your inherent worth.

This energetic structure of the contracts is like a vortex that supports your automatic responses. You remain linked to the people you originally experienced those exchanges with, through invisible threads in the unified field called 'aka cords'. Aka is a word derived from the Hawaiian sacred teachings of Huna or 'secret knowledge'. It can be described as a sticky, elastic substance, which connects each of us and relates to the string theory, posed by quantum physicists. The string theory, often called the 'theory of everything', suggests that all objects in our universe are composed of vibrating filaments (strings) and membranes (branes) of energy. Aka threads connect you to everyone and everything.

The more contact you have with a person, the more the thread builds until they become braided together to form aka cords. When you have a strong aka cord connection with someone, you strengthen your telepathic communication and it also becomes easier to become 'emotionally hooked'. This is one of the reasons why certain members of your family have a tendency to 'push your buttons', even at the best of times. The exchange in the relationship is not just cerebral or even emotional – it is energetic.

With parent and child, aka cords are like 'apron strings', built on an exchange of emotionally charged thoughts. These subtle, yet influential invisible threads transmit information via tiny impulses through that psychic network – until you sever the ties. Not physically but energetically. Your aim is to lift the quality of the exchange in your relationships – not remove the person from your life. That is, of course, unless the relationship is destructive.

Once you have taken your power back, you are at liberty to choose and renegotiate your contract, based on an equitable exchange.

To understand how the contracts and scripts play out, let's take a look beneath the facade of Marianne's world. She originally approached me when her highly organized, glamorous life started to crumble. At which point her demeanor dramatically shifted.

Her bubbly, polite persona was tainted with anxiety, resentment and anger. The tension between Marianne and her husband Carl was quickly mounting. As a result, maintaining her mask of 'niceness' had become progressively more difficult. Carl was a highly ambitious executive who had the reputation of being arrogant, cocky and insensitive in both his business and his personal affairs. For him Marianne was a 'trophy bride' based on her ability to turn heads, together with her kind and generous nature. By contrast Carl was a loud and boisterous man whose energy often left observers feeling affronted.

From a very young age, Marianne entertained visions of living a full and prosperous life. With a portfolio of real estate, a successful business and a new baby daughter, her wish list was almost complete. There was one prominent component missing: a faithful loving partner. Carl had recently been accused of sexual harassment, which sent Marianne into a tailspin. The volume was turned up on that drama when Carl assaulted his young secretary's fiancé when he angrily challenged his integrity.

Most of Marianne's friends were well aware of Carl's womanizing and wondered why she'd put up with him. When they told her she deserved more, she simply made excuses for his behavior and changed the subject. Although she had chosen to turn a blind eye for five years, burying her head in the sand was no longer an option. Carl was now up on criminal charges, which made it far too difficult to hide her shame.

His lurid conduct was reminiscent of her father's behavior and the incident released a flood of painful memories from her childhood. This intense outplay of Soul-Speak presented the perfect opportunity for Marianne to uncover her psychic contracts and change her life-script.

She had been playing the role of loyal, devoted, partner and the 'perfect wife'. She'd maintained that impeccable profile despite her husband's brash behavior, which was identical to her father's. Marianne had grown up defending herself from her father's destructive cynicism as he accused her of "being too big for her boots, or warned her to 'get off her high horse" He complained that she had her head in the clouds and needed to do more chores. Whenever she asked him for money, he simply said, "Earn it".

Marianne's father wanted her to limit her own potential and understand that nothing would be given to her just because she was who she was. He believed she had to work hard for anything she wanted and that her self belief and confidence were dangerous and arrogant.

Rather than accept this view, Marianne rebelled against her father's grim forecasts, setting out to prove him wrong. That one noteworthy objective became the strongest clause in their psychic contract. When she wrote the following words in her journal, they struck accord at the depths of her being. 'I will promise to spend the rest of my life proving to you that I am worthy of your attention and good enough to be loved.' She knew, despite the strength of her spirit, as a young child her heart had been broken.

At the tender age of nine, her father refused to attend a celebration at the town hall honoring Marianne for her outstanding performance in gymnastics. From the age of five, when she first began training, he never once took an interest in her talent. Her way of shielding herself from the pain of defeat was to pledge, 'I will never rely on you for anything.'

Her joy of winning a trophy was tainted with sadness, with the cold absence of her father. That defining moment gave rise to a list of sub-clauses that she used to bolster her esteem. – 'I will never need you', 'I will always work hard to get what I want' and 'You will never destroy my dreams'.

One of the declarations that Marianne made with her father became glaringly obvious in her relationship with Carl. When he threatened to ruin her if she left him, she simply said, "I will never let you control me."

Marianne's father was a tyrant who held a tight reign on everyone in the family, which is why his daughter became fiercely independent. Her mother would often tiptoe around her father, always putting on a brave face despite her underlying sorrow. She was an extremely compliant woman who lived in fear of her husband's nasty temper. To protect her daughter, she told her not to agitate or challenge her father in order to keep the peace. Trailing her mother's footsteps, Marianne agreed to the following – 'I will never answer back' therefore 'I will forfeit my right to speak up' and 'I will keep things to myself.' As a consequence she added, 'I agree to deny myself tenderness and closeness'. Consequently Marianne promised to be well mannered, gentle and polite to avoid conflict, wearing a cheerful face no matter what was going on.

Marianne was the light in her mother's world. She offered her daughter support and encouragement by constantly reminding her how talented and pretty she was. In exchange Marianne agreed to always take care of her. One of the key clauses in their psychic contract was, 'I promise to never complain' That declaration of intent was followed by, 'I will ignore my own feelings and agree to never burden you. Above all, I will never disappoint you'.

That final decree was solidly put in place during a defining moment on the night of Marianne's 16th birthday. In a drunken stupor, her father callously embarrassed her in front of her friends.

Marianne was so incensed that she lost her temper and stormed out of the front door of the house with her father's car keys. She pulled out of the driveway with him threatening to beat the living daylights out of her. Instead, he turned his rage on her mother, slapping her hard across the face. He blamed her for being too soft with his children and spoiling them rotten.

When Marianne finally went home to discover the aftermath of her father's rampage, she was shocked to find her mother's face bruised and swollen; riddled with guilt and shame, she felt responsible for her mother's pain. Crying tears of remorse, she vowed to make it up to her by never letting her down again. That was the night that Marianne agreed to forfeit her right to be fully acknowledged, taking care not to upset or anger others.

Although Marianne was a powerful negotiator regarding business deals, when it came to affairs of the heart she had a difficult time declaring her rights. Her head and her heart were at odds and she needed to reinstate her balance. Although it took the crisis with Carl to snap her out of her slumber, she knew things had to change. To finally end her taxing marriage, she had to break one central clause in her psychic contracts, 'I will never put myself first.'

Marianne set her intention to make her happiness a priority and start expressing herself. After destroying her old contracts and writing a new script, she turned her back on Carl and left with her daughter. She declared, from that point on, any relationship she had with a man needed to reflect mutual respect.

A year later she moved in with John, who treated her with care and tenderness. They shared their personal dreams and formed a common vision, which they jointly took steps to create. Based on the work Marianne did with her scripts, she knew how important it was that they both express their needs and be willing to respond to them equally. As a result, they made formal agreements, which they lovingly upheld. Successfully creating a solid base for a wonderful future, Marianne and John are still happily together ten years later. Their partnership is a testimony to how honesty and communication are crucial in any good relationship.

Marianne's story clearly illustrates the value of setting our intentions and monitoring where our attention goes. She is now a great ambassadress for authentic self-expression and is committed to speaking her truth. Love and fear can't exist in the same space; therefore we have to be clear where our commitment lies. We choose the game, then write the rules and invite our partners to play. It is important we stop looking at our past to gauge what is possible in our relationships and continue to revise our scripts. Before we begin that process, we all need to ask ourselves how much love we are willing to experience and how much of ourselves we are willing to share.

Charting your course

Write your intention in your journal. Because you will be working specifically with your contracts and scripts, use a declaration that aligns with reclaiming your personal power.

Perhaps it is something like:

> **'During this level of the course I intend to monitor who I give my power to and graciously reclaim it.'**

Or you may prefer something more direct like:

> **'As I progress through this level of the course I intend to break free from the shackles of my past and take my power back from . . . '**

Or

> **'I intend to be conscious of what script I am living into and change my character.'**

Choose statements that you are genuinely willing to abide by. Make your declaration of intent in the presence of your Higher Self and Soul, so you know you will make every effort to stand by your word.

Write this **Pocket Affirmation** *in your journal and post it in a prominent position to refer to as your daily mantra.*

'I have free will and claim my right to choose my destiny. I am powerful, I am loving and I am true to myself.'

Write the Key Words **Autonomy versus Conformity** *in your journal and contemplate them on a daily basis. Become conscious of which of the two you align with more often, to help you assess where you give your power away.*

Do the meditation for this level for a minimum of 15 minutes at least once before moving onto the next level. This is an extremely important step. You may want to record any insights in your journal.

The process

The first step to uncovering your scripts and contracts is to pinpoint the defining moments that helped to shape your character. Those destiny points on the Map of the Soul highlight your fears and will help you distinguish the boundaries you set up to protect you from being hurt. They are the incidents where you denied your true potential and surrendered your personal power. They serve as clues to where you need to deepen the relationship you have with yourself and reinstate your sense of worth.

You need to be able to look back at your past and know that you have retrieved your power from everyone you have given it to. That will allow you to fulfill your heart's desires without subconsciously believing you need someone else to endorse your dreams or give you permission to have what you want. You are your own adviser and the caretaker of your own Soul – you are the one who ultimately chooses what you experience. So from now on, choose wisely, based on what you feel in your heart is appropriate for you.

Watch your negative Ego and underlying fears throughout this process. You will feel a certain amount of resistance based on the fact that your contracts have kept you safe since you were a child. They don't just exist in your mind, they are held in place in your energy field, which has a magnetic pull. Keep in mind that they have also stood in the way of you being fully empowered. Consider the cost of keeping the psychic contracts in place. Not just in regard to your having the things you want, like wealth, a certain type of relationship, children or a particular career. Look at what the cost is regarding your relationship with yourself – specifically your Soul.

What have you forfeited in those exchanges and agreements that is an aspect of your nature – your pride, your dignity, your freedom, your beauty, your power, your uniqueness, your creativity? Look for what you have denied. They are precious parts of your Soul that are there to be claimed.

Stretching beyond your comfort zone can be challenging; yet it is imperative to growth. You may be confronted by a fear of not being loved or accepted if you change your agreements. If this is the case consider the conditions of your contract and ask yourself if they honestly serve you. To truly honor your feelings, you always need to keep your best interests at heart and consider your highest choices. Be mindful of who you are playing out in your scripts and look closely at the exchange in the relationship. They will either be conditional or liberal – restricting your expression or fostering your growth.

The antidote to a restrictive script is to tear it up and create a new map by making new agreements with yourself. That new contract is a sacred covenant you enter into with your Soul – a pledge to become more of your True Self. You have not just made these psychic contracts with others – you have ultimately made them with yourself. The power always rests with you if you are willing to claim it.

Write your answers to the following exercises in your journal.

EXERCISE 10 – PART A:
Defining Moments – Childhood

For this particular exercise sit quietly with your journal and formally ask your subconscious and Higher Self to work with you. Your aim is to find an incident in your childhood between the ages of four to ten, where you experienced intense fear. You may have also felt intense sorrow, shame, loneliness or despair.

Once you indentify the feelings, sense the underlying hurt – feelings of being rejected, abandoned, betrayed or humiliated. Then ask yourself what decision you made about yourself, for example: I am bad, I am weak,

I am stupid, I am ugly etc. Cast your thoughts and feelings back to your childhood, and allow the memories to drift through your mind.

You may find an unexpected event pops up out of the blue. If you find it difficult to remember your childhood, look for small cameos of things or objects you had around you when you were little and move with the flow of your imagination. Or think about the things you liked to do. Once you open that file in your subconscious the information will just come to you.

Write a short synopsis of the story that describes one or two of your most significant defining moments when you experienced intense constrictive emotions, including hurt and fear.

1. I remember when I was _____years of age, I felt afraid when _____ happened.
2. When that happened, I felt hurt because _____and specifically I felt (rejected, abandoned, betrayed or humiliated)_____ .

The outcome was I saw myself as_____

EXERCISE 10 – PART B:

Defining Moments – Adolescence.

Repeat the same exercise in relationship to your adolescent years. Your aim is to find an incident between the ages of eleven and seventeen, where you experienced intense fear and hurt. This will pinpoint the time of your Soul's wounding.

Write a short synopsis of the story that describes the most significant defining moment when you were a teenager.

1. I remember when I was _____years of age, I felt afraid when _____ happened.
2. When that happened, I felt hurt because _____and specifically I felt (rejected, abandoned, betrayed or humiliated) _____ .

The outcome was I saw myself as_____

EXERCISE 11 – PART A:

Uncovering your Negative Psychic Contracts

Your aim is identify the disempowering agreements you made with your guardians, teachers or caretakers when you were a child. They are people who had a strong impact and influence on your development. The most significant would be your mother and father – alternatively a grandparent, older sibling or relative who played a similar role.

Do a separate contract for each individual. Your contract with your father may be very different from the one you have with your mother or perhaps a grandparent who took on their role. Look for three things –

What you agreed to

What you forfeited your right to

What part of your character you denied in that process.

Your Contract

1. Note your guardian's name at the top of a page in your journal. Reflect on the defining moment from your childhood.

2. Write a first draft of the agreements you made with that person without editing. Get in touch with your feelings and let the information flow out onto the page. Write one, two or three pages if necessary. Just make sure you don't leave anything out!

   I agree to _____ and therefore forfeit my right to_____ and agree to deny my _____

3. Add to that same first draft by reflecting on the defining moment from your teenage years. Write down the concrete declarations you made at the time. They are clearly defined absolutes. Make sure to get in touch with your feelings and let the information come to you.

   I agree to _____and therefore forfeit my right to_____and agree to deny_____.

4. Take a clean sheet of paper that is separate from your journal that you will eventually destroy. Review what you have written and draw up a formal agreement that looks like a legal document with specific clauses. You can use the template provided or create your own template. Fill it in neatly and sign the bottom.

Completed Example:

Contract with Father

I agree to *follow in your footsteps and never be better than you.* Therefore I forfeit my right to *stand out in the world and be acknowledged.* I therefore agree to deny *my uniqueness*

Negative Contract and Agreement (sample)

This agreement is made between_____and _____to

form a co-operative partnership based on the following conditions:

ARTICLE I.

1. The nature of our relationship is _____.

I _____known as the first party, agree to co-operate with _____

referred to as the second party by adhering to the following terms.

I, the first party, promise to _____. As a sub-clause to the

agreement, I also agree to forfeit my right to _____.

To uphold the original I also agree to deny my_____.

ARTICLE 2.

I the first party promise to _____. As a sub-clause to the

agreement, I also agree to forfeit my right to _____.

To uphold the original I also agree to deny my_____.

ARTICLE 3.

I the first party promise to _____. As a sub-clause to the

agreement, I also agree to forfeit my right to _____.

To uphold the original I also agree to deny my_____.

(CONTINUE ARTICLES UNTIL COMPLETION)

Signed by _____Date: _____

Breaking your Psychic Contracts

Once you have completed your formal contract, put it in a safe place.

Ask your Higher Self and Soul for permission to break the contract over the next few days.

For the next three days, look for a distinct sign through Soul-Speak about contracts or agreements. It could show up as a headline on a newspaper that states something like 'U.S.A signs new treaty with China.' Or perhaps a television news announcement like 'Tiger Woods signs new contract Nike . . .'. Or it may a line that stands out in a movie.

You may be sitting in a cafe and overhear someone say, 'My divorce papers just came through, I am free.'

One of my clients had a dream where her mother showed up and told her it was time for them to change their contract! Others have shared that a parent has literally called them and suggested they change something about their relationship.

Once you get a clear sign, the next step is to do the meditation for this level. If you don't get a sign within three days, go back over what you have written to find what you left out. Add to it and go through the process again until you get a clear sign.

The last step is to rip up the contract, burn it safely and dispose of the remains.

EXERCISE 12:

Write you Soul's Covenant.

Your aim in this exercise is to replace your psychic contracts with a pledge to your Soul. Sit quietly and make a declaration of intent that you will honor yourself in particular ways going forward. Consider statements that counteract the clauses in your old agreements. State precisely what you promise to uphold in the relationship with yourself.

Do not write anything you are not willing to uphold. A pledge to your Soul needs to be made earnestly.

Covenant

I _____ offer my solemn vow to uphold the following agreement from
this day forward.
In the presence of my Soul, I promise to honor myself by_____
_____ As long as I shall live.

Signed: _____Date:

Marianne's Completed Covenant:

I, *Marianne Martin,* offer my solemn vow to uphold the following
agreement from this day forward.

In the presence of my Soul, I promise to honor myself by *supporting my
goals and cherishing my dreams. I promise to acknowledge and be grateful for
my talents and use them. Celebrate the beauty in the world. Use the gift of my
creativity. I pledge to be honest and open in all of my relationships, maintaining
my integrity. I will muster the courage to directly state my preferences. I promise
to nurture myself on a daily basis. I will develop the level of intimacy in my
relationships, knowing I am good enough to be loved. I promise to be humble
enough to receive more and give more.* As long as I shall live.

Signed: Marianne Martin   Date: 10.10.10

EXERCISE 13 – PART A:
Writing your Negative Scripts

The goal of this exercise is to clarify the script you have being living and define the character that you have been playing out. This will shine a spotlight on the stumbling blocks you repeatedly face and where you give your power away. Pinpoint the players and their objective. Who do you write into your scripts? Are they playboys, princes, damsels in distress, villains, martyrs, victims, dominators or weaklings? The script will reflect your old contracts and agreements – who have you given your power to, who, aside from you, do you allow to decree who you are and how much you receive?

Review your life and choose an archetype or fairy-tale character that fits your life story.

Be creative and write a short script or synopsis that portrays the repetitive challenges and pitfalls of the character.

Once you have identified a clearly defined thread, sit back and read through the script until you can clearly acknowledge that you have chosen that path with blame to none. To truly change the ending, you need to be willing to claim your power as the creator of your reality and let everyone from your past off the hook!

Have fun with this exercise. Be creative and turn up the volume on the melodrama. Choose an archetype or fairy-tale character that fits your saga to emphasize the fact that you choose the roles you play and make up your own story. Remain compassionate toward yourself as you write, rather than being judgmental. The point of this exercise is to help you see how easy it is to follow an invisible script and recite the cue cards. It will highlight your automatic expectations and responses.

EXERCISE 13 – PART B:

Updating Your Script

The next part of this exercise is to develop the substance of your character and then create a twist in the story. Alter the behavior of your key characters, introduce some new, inspiring players and change the ending!

With a clear outline of your story in mind, use your imagination to create a scenario that would alter your character to such a degree that it changes the storyline and points to a different more positive ending. Then write a new ending that aligns with your heart's desires. Remember, you can have anything, be anyone or do anything, with harm to none. You have free will.

Marianne's Completed Exercise:

It was clear that Marianne had suffered in silence, which doused the joy in her heart. She had secretly wished the ogre, who kept her imprisoned, would release his stronghold to set her free. She attempted to see his goodness, knowing he was once an innocent child. Throughout that quest, she had denied her own beauty and truth, which was now no longer an option. Marianne knew she had deceived herself and felt a deep sense of remorse. In that poignant moment, the stark reality hit of how much pain she had put herself through.

She knew the key to her happiness lay in her own hands and not in the pocket of the ogre. Packing her suitcase, she vowed from this day forward to never betray herself ever again. As she drove through the steel gates of the property onto the open road, she knew she was finally free to start a new life.

As the days progressed Marianne grew more confident, celebrating all that her life offered. With her newfound courage and passion, she claimed her right to be loved and acknowledged, despite the opinions of others. It was only a matter of time before the ogre became a distant memory. Finally knowing her worth, Marianne attracted a new partner who pledged to honor their relationship and hold it sacred ...

MEDITATION

The intention behind this meditation is for you to disconnect from the effects of the psychic contracts you made with your parents or guardians. Keep in mind that the agreements exist in your energy field until you take your power back.

You may choose to make a note of what you forfeited or denied and wish to claim back.

Find a comfortable position and begin to relax. Gently close your eyes.

Focus on your breathing and empty your mind of all thoughts. Take three deep breaths and exhale slowly.

Imagine one of your parents standing in front of you. Visualize fine cords or threads connecting the two of you at the following points –

- A point at the top of your head
- The centre of your forehead
- Your throat
- Your heart
- Your solar plexus
- Your pelvic region
- The base of your spine.

Imagine that you are having a conversation with the person and declare your choice to end your contract. Tell them you are reinstating your authority to choose for yourself. You may wish to specifically declare which rights and qualities you want to reclaim.

Build the energy of your desire and will until you feel it intensely. Now cut or sever the cords connecting you at each point. You can imagine a knife, scissors or a sword – just break them. Place your hand over each of the points of your body and feel your energy returning as you breathe deeply.

Thank them for the wisdom and lessons you have learnt from your experiences. Imagine you are bowing to each other. Then watch the person fade into the background. Repeat the exercise with your next guardian.

Once you have completed the ritual – take a deep breath and gently bring yourself out of the meditation.

Your checklist

1. Did you write in your journal on a regular basis to observe your thoughts and feelings?
2. Did you record any Soul-Speak?
3. Have you logged your insights, goals and aspirations?
4. Were you mindful of your intention?
5. Did you take time to contemplate the Divine Truth and the two Key Words?
6. Have you been using your Pocket Affirmation on a regular basis?
7. Have you taken the time to do your meditation to break the psychic contracts?
8. Have you done your exercises and logged them?
9. Have you been conscious of your script and willing to change the ending so it supports your Heart's Desire?
10. If you haven't done any or all of these things then ask yourself - what stopped you?

You may be going into denial or avoidance around the topic for this particular level of self-discovery – what has your Ego been telling you? Those conversations reflect your limited beliefs about yourself. CHALLENGE THEM! Remember – your heart's desires are at stake.

LEVEL

6

During this level of the course you will uncover the treasures and truths of your Shadow, which will allow you to claim more of your power and beauty. There is nothing missing within you. Each of your veiled character traits is a gift waiting to be discovered. By learning to embrace your Shadow, you will finally realize you are 'good enough', knowing that you are whole and complete.

Retrieving the Depths of Soul and Spirit – Shadow

DIVINE TRUTH: You are whole and complete – there is nothing missing inside of you.

KEY WORDS: Wholeness versus Fragmentation

You are whole and complete. If you are willing to embrace all aspects of who you are without reservation, you will fragment your energy and dissociate from parts of your Soul or Essence.

'It is futile to ostracize the parts of us that we find undesirable because they exist as aspects of our Soul. We simply need to accept them and realize that we are an aspect of All That Is.'

In Jungian psychology, the 'Shadow' or 'Shadow aspect' is a part of the unconscious that holds the denied parts of the self. It consists of your repressed weaknesses and shortcomings along with your radiance. The Shadow is made up of what we have been taught or conditioned to deny. The Dark Shadow contains the aspects of your nature you deem as unacceptable – the darkness or ugliness you won't admit to. The Light Shadow is made up of the power and beauty you pretend you don't have – aspects of your nature you have dismissed by disregarding your worth. It holds your true spirituality and the lost depth of your Soul and Spirit.

From a spiritual perspective, your Shadow is the aspect of you that is a reciprocal or companion for your Soul. It is a face of the Soul that is born with you and trails after you, picking up the things you drop as you go along your way. It holds those denied parts of your nature, discarded by the child and dispersed by the frightened adolescent, waiting to be retrieved.

They are the pieces of you that you refuse to own at present, but eventually will – as a part of your Soul's Destiny. Both the light and dark human qualities that you reject remain in your Shadow until you are willing to accept and integrate them. Your Shadow consists of aspects of your consciousness – it is a part of your Soul. Therefore part of your Soul's purpose is to retrieve those lost parts of self and bring them into the light. Doing the shadow work is an imperative part of your spiritual growth. Done earnestly, it will allow you to make peace with all parts of yourself and finally recognize that you are whole and complete.

Each human characteristic exists within all of us. Based on the fact we have free will, we each choose which particular qualities we own, develop and express. It is futile to ostracize the parts of us that we find undesirable because they exist as aspects of our consciousness. We simply need to accept them and realize that we are an aspect of All That Is and that we choose our disposition.

We are the ones who ultimately label and dissect parts of our nature. The Shadow is neither bad nor good, right nor wrong – we are perfect and pure in essence. By accepting all parts of ourselves, we acknowledge our full potential and true heritage, which is an empowering place to be. Otherwise we continue to live in fear of being rejected and overcompensate in certain areas to make up for others.

We live in a world of polarity and yet we are all ultimately heading for a state of oneness – a level where no separation exists. To attain that position as an individual, we need to harmonize our energy by denouncing segregation. If we continue to renounce parts of our nature, we deny the presence of love, which is the thread that creates unity.

Love is always present; we are the ones who move away from that State. Ultimately that fall from grace is based on fear and judgment. The Ego is the part of our nature that casts those negative decrees. Our Higher Self and Soul love us unconditionally, maintaining that commitment under all circumstances.

Each negative quality has a positive counterpart that balances the other. They each have their place in the grand scheme of things when considered as a part of the whole. Therefore to resolve all internal conflict, we need to be at peace with every single human quality or characteristic – rejecting none. By owning and mastering all of those qualities, we dismantle the separation that exists with our Soul. The more enlightened we become, the more the darker sides of our nature are illuminated. From that vantage point, our vision of who we are expands and we know we have nothing to fear.

Your Light and Dark Shadow started to form in your early childhood, especially during defining moments. As you progressed to your teenage years, that process was compounded by feelings of guilt, shame, fear and hurt. During your development, you concluded certain parts of you were valuable, lovable and acceptable, and leant on those to build your character.

By contrast, those that you deemed to be bad, wrong or useless were cast aside or dismissed. You were intimidated by some qualities and inspired by others, holding up invisible scorecards. This is why your Shadow holds the clue to all the conditions you place around love and acceptance.

Those denied qualities that reside in your Dark Shadow have their place when tempered by their polar opposites, which is why it is so important that you embrace your Light Shadow to initiate that balance. Yet as a collective, many of us have attached negative connotations to positive qualities such as beauty, power, magnificence and greatness, associating them with arrogance, coldness, vanity or conceit. We dim our light to make people more comfortable or to avoid their jealousy, envy, judgment or criticism.

At other times we turn down the volume on our splendor to avoid being used or abused. As an example, for some people being sensual can be an asset. For others it can be dangerous, indulgent or even offensive. Being spontaneous and adventurous can be seen as fun and exciting or construed as irresponsible, disrespectful or even recklessness. It is all based on your point of perception and the meaning you attach to things.

When you can own being ugly and know you are beautiful, you are free to be yourself. If you own being weak and know you can be brilliant, you can remain humble. It is important to find that point of balance, denying neither, embracing both. The point of power exists in knowing you are simply free to be who you choose to be. Otherwise you will be driven by certain fears and remain self-conscious in different areas.

There are times we all take on roles to fit in or stand out. Just keep a watch on your negative Ego and where you are coming from in your positioning. For example, if your underlying intention is to be serious to avoid being seen as superficial or frivolous, you will cast the playful parts of you aside. If you consistently choose to be self-sacrificing, unassuming or dutiful in order to be seen as 'good', your vivacity and uniqueness will rescind to the Shadow. False modesty has little to do with goodness; it diminishes your inherent worth and validates Ego. Statements such as, 'I don't have a mean bone in my body', 'I'm not good with money', 'I'm not creative', 'I have no imagination', 'I'm never rebellious' or 'I'm not demanding'. Keep in mind that the 'I am' along with 'I am not' statements dissect your wholeness. There are increments and degrees or everything; in certain circumstances you could be any of those things.

If you run away from parts of your nature out of fear, they will end up running your life. To avoid being seen in a particular way, you will be driven to do the opposite. Avoiding being 'dumb and stupid' could drive that person to be a workaholic, not take vacations and be forced to always do things of substance rather than having fun.

The irony is, with Shadow everything is subjective. That person could also be seen as 'dumb and stupid' for not taking time to enjoy life and consider their health! If they swing the pendulum to that degree, they will risk being controlling, righteous and arrogant.

People are not inherently bad; they just make bad choices and decisions. They are inherently good and that goodness always remains a part of them. It can be denied but it cannot die. Even people like Hitler and Saddam Hussein, who appeared for most of us as Dark Shadow, had their strengths. Through the eyes of their followers, they were indicative of Light Shadow, reflecting the qualities of being powerful, unique and influential, just to name a few. Tyrants will continue to show up in our world until we make peace with the tyrant within ourselves, at which point, our denied Shadow will no longer bleed through the cracks and crevices into our daily lives, bubbling up from the unconscious.

So how do you identify your Shadow? If you find yourself denying that you have particular characteristics then that is a distinct indication.

The hardest qualities to own are the ones you associate with painful experiences where you have been hurt or felt shame. Incidents where you have been rejected, abandoned, betrayed or humiliated. If for any reason you hold onto those grievances, and refuse to take your power back, you will always blame someone else and remain trapped. You will then build evidence to support your claims and justify your position. That is why it is imperative that you break your psychic contracts and reclaim the denied parts of your Soul. They are precious portions of your essence that allow you to be fully self-expressed.

The easiest way to detect Dark Shadow is to pay attention when someone 'pushes your buttons' and you find yourself automatically judging them. It is the same if you have an allergic reaction to someone's mannerisms and you become reactive. The aspects of their personality that irritate you will reveal what you don't like about yourself.

By contrast, your Light Shadow will be reflected in the people in your world that you are in awe of or put on a pedestal, wishing you had the same qualities. Your parents, family members and siblings will always represent Shadow – both Dark and Light. Look to the intimates in your world, along with your friends and colleagues for clues, as well as the reoccurring patterns around betrayal abandonment, humiliation or rejection.

These cameos will keep reappearing as Life-speak and Dream-speak to gain your attention. They are projections, which offer you clues from your Soul. Until you fully embrace those aspects of consciousness, without reluctance, pity or judgment, your Shadow self will haunt you until you finally claim it.

For any of us to love unconditionally, we first need to accept ourselves fully. Yet most of us find that concept extremely confronting. Many people even believe that if they accept themselves, they will remain flawed and never change. However, the opposite is true. If you are willing to look at all of your human qualities, both light and dark, and embrace each and every one of them, you will find a point of balance.

Shadow Play in Relationships

There are few of us who have reached a level of self-love that allows us to consistently uphold our confidence without wavering. Most of us feel incomplete in some way. Whenever we search for someone else to fill that void we disregard our true worth. Until we retrieve the hidden parts of our Soul from the Shadow, we will never feel completely satisfied.

If we enter into a relationship to compensate for our own shortcomings, we will view the person, rather than the relationship, as a source of security or pleasure. In reality, our partnerships merely reflect the relationship we have with ourselves, and serve as a platform for our self-expression. It can be easy to fall into the trap of thinking that having a partner will make us feel better about ourselves, but unless we choose a relationship based on preference, rather than need, we are liable to come unstuck. This was the case with Maggie who relied on Bill to make up for the parts of her she thought were missing, which led to a list of compromises.

She entered the relationship with the underlying intention of bolstering her limitations, denying her full potential. Maggie had a core belief that she needed a partner to become whole and complete. She was gentle and yielding, which drew her to men who were strong, dynamic and highly ambitious, who played out the role of protector and provider. She had fought most of her life to maintain the profile of being soft, demure and loving to such a degree she had jeopardized her potency of will.

Her resistance to moving beyond her restrictive image diminished the masculine side of her nature. Maggie's fear of being hard and cold watered down her passion and vigor, leaving he to rely on others to take the lead.

Bill was a strategic thinker who was disciplined, athletic and driven, whereas Maggie was nurturing, sensitive and playful. Maggie made the mistake of looking for a partner to 'complete' rather than 'complement' her, which eventually led to conflict. She started resenting Bill for being aloof and rigid at times, which were qualities she had avoided being most of her life.

Bill originally showed the gentler sides of his nature, until he lost his patience with Maggie's passive mannerisms. He started to resent the fact she relied on him to make most of the decisions and rarely instigated anything new. Once the physical chemistry began to wane in their relationship, Bill and Maggie mirrored each other's faults and weaknesses, inciting a round of 'Shadow play'. Bill expected Maggie to be more outgoing and adventurous like him and Maggie wanted Bill to be more tender and affectionate, like her.

When Maggie desired more from Bill, she turned up the volume on her feminine charms, which simply aggravated him. The lighter qualities he originally admired in her became distorted; he began to see her as weak, insecure and needy. Bill's thoughtful, gallant persona became tough, harsh and unyielding, which only made Maggie more submissive.

Alarmed by her dwindling pride, she decided to come and see me. She had been through a similar scenario with her previous boyfriend and was finally ready to change her patterns. When I suggested to Maggie she claim the strengths she sought in her partners, her immediate response was 'I have never been good at those things.'

The truth was Maggie was resistant to being assertive based on her fear of being aggressive, all under the guise of wanting to remain feminine. It wasn't as if she wasn't capable of strengthening her will, she was just terrified. To quote Maggie, 'I couldn't stand ending up like my mother.'

Maggie's mother was strikingly beautiful and the perfect socialite wife. Priding herself on being a perfectionist, her life revolved around pleasing her husband, fulfilling his every request. Maggie's father enjoyed the attention and paraded her proudly on the end of his arm. He was a handsome, affluent man, idealized by his wife and daughter who placed him on a pedestal. All of that changed the day that Maggie's mother discovered he was having an affair.

More than a brief encounter, the affair had been going for several years. As the grim details turned her mother's face white, Maggie watched her father drop to his knees and beg for forgiveness. Like a wounded wildcat her mother viciously turned on him and said she was leaving. From that day forward, eight-year-old Maggie's fairytale life slowly came to an end.

Deeply wounded, her mother became cold and bitter, drowning her sorrows behind an elegant façade. Watching both of her parents' battle through a harrowing divorce, Maggie sided with her father, relating to him as the sweet and sensitive one. Labeling her mother selfish, she vowed to never forgive her. Absorbing the impact of her mother's aggression, Maggie equated defiance with destruction, dismissing that part of her into the Shadow. She made the mistake of swinging the pendulum, from one extreme to the other, becoming compliant.

As a result of repressing her initiative and dynamism, Maggie diminished the vibrancy of her Spirit. Curiously enough, Bill had done the exact opposite. He was intimidated by the thought of being sensitive and nurturing, which he labeled as weak. As a result, he denied a large chunk of his Soul and relied heavily on the intensity of his Spirit. They were a 'perfect match', playing out complete opposites.

At times we attract people into our world as powerful catalysts to facilitate change. Bill ignited a spark of passion in Maggie, but it was up to her to keep that flame alive. It was also up to Bill to nurture the gentler sides of his nature, which Maggie initially inspired. If a couple continue to grow together by claiming more of their Light Shadow and accepting more of the Dark, they will progressively build a deep and harmonious union.

Our relationships offer us nourishment and inspiration. The depth of intimacy in those exchanges indicates precisely how much of ourselves we are willing to reveal and how much of the other person we are willing to discover. The only way that we can strengthen a relationship is by continuing to search for deeper understanding of each other and develop the level of closeness and tenderness. Because we are still in the process of learning more about ourselves as individuals, this needs to be an ongoing practice.

'Freedom of expression is based on trust and confidence. When we feel as though there is something missing in our world, we need to open up to discovering and sharing more of ourselves. '

Charting your course

Write your intention in your journal. Because you will be working specifically with your Shadow, use a declaration that aligns with reclaiming the lost parts of your Soul.

Perhaps it is something like:

'During this level of the course I will be mindful of which aspects of my nature I deny – both light and dark.'

Or you may prefer something more direct like:

'As I progress through this level of the course I intend to reclaim the following positive qualities that I currently deny.'

Or

'I will pay attention to the people I am in awe of and embrace the qualities they exhibit within myself.'

Choose statements that you are genuinely willing to abide by. Make your declaration of intent in the presence of your Higher Self and Soul, so you know you will make every effort to stand by your word.

Write this **Pocket Affirmation** *in your journal and post it in a prominent position to refer to as your daily mantra.*

'I am whole and complete – there is nothing missing within me. I am a magnificent reflection of my Soul and am becoming all I can be.'

Write the Key Words **Wholeness versus Fragmentation** *in your journal and contemplate them on a daily basis. Become conscious of which of the two you align with more often, to help you assess where you give your power away.*

Do the meditation for this level for a minimum of 15 minutes at least three times before moving onto the next level. You may want to record any insights in your journal.

The process

You are well equipped to handle anything you face in the world – if you are willing to trust your internal resources.

Remember, as an aspect of All That Is, there is nothing missing in you. It is just a matter of perceiving yourself from a more expansive point of view. By exploring your Shadow Self, you can move toward happiness, wholeness and freedom. By accepting all parts of yourself wholeheartedly, you will finally acknowledge the great truth that you are worthy of being fully loved. The key is to relate to your self as a multi-dimensional being with a myriad of faces.

There are treasures waiting to be discovered in your Shadow – denied aspects of your power and beauty. The benefit to owning your Shadow is that you are no longer afraid of it. If you are courageous enough to face both the dark and the light parts of you, you will eventually master them all. You can then comfortably choose who you want to be, without inhibition.

Write your answers to the following exercises in your journal.

EXERCISE 14 – PART A:

Illuminating the Dark Shadow

The first step to uncovering your darker side is to pinpoint the people in your life who play out your Shadow. Review the following players in your world and take time to reflect on the qualities they exhibit which you refuse to own. Look specifically for traits that trigger a negative reaction and evoke an intense emotional response.

To find clues, look for areas where you hear yourself saying, 'I am not like that.'

Reviewing your parents, make a list of their negative qualities that stand out. Which of those qualities do you own and which are you afraid of or deny?

Do the same with your siblings.

Repeat the exercise with the 'intimates' in your life (friends and lovers) that reflect the Shadow.

Repeat the exercise with the 'players' or people that keep showing up in your life that reflect the Shadow.

EXERCISE 14 – PART B:

Illuminating the Light Shadow

Review the following players in your world and take time to reflect on the positive qualities they exhibit that you deny. Look specifically for traits that incite awe and evoke an intense emotional response.

To find clues, look for areas where you hear yourself saying, 'I wish I was more like that.'

Reviewing your parents, make a list of their positive qualities that stand out. Which of those qualities do you own and which do you deny?

Do the same with your siblings.

Repeat the exercise with the 'intimates' in your life (friends and lovers) that reflect the Shadow.

Repeat the exercise with the 'players' or people that keep showing up in your life that reflect the Shadow.

EXERCISE 15 – PART A:

Uncovering your Shadow Self

The aim of this exercise is to clarify what you specifically dumped in your Shadow. Look closely at defining moments when you experienced intense fear, hurt or shame to see what labels you attached to certain parts of you. Did you play certain parts of you down to make others feel more comfortable or to avoid their wrath? Were you told you were greedy, selfish, pushy, demanding, cruel, vain, mean or tough? Did being beautiful or brilliant pose a threat based on others being jealous, envious or confronted in some way? Were others annoyed by the thought that you were better than them? Did you feel awkward or different based on your talents or strengths?

Look at a few of the defining moments in your childhood and adolescence and make note of the specific qualities you dumped in the Shadow at the time. Make two lists – Negative or Dark and Positive or Light.

EXERCISE 15 – PART B:

Uncovering your Shadow Self

The goal of this exercise is to summarize your list of Shadow traits to see which have the most influence. By integrating those first, it is likely to have a domino effect. Look over your list of positive and negative traits and highlight the ones that really stand out by asking the following questions.

Which parts of your Shadow Self do you despise or regard as worthless?

Which of the Dark qualities on your list do you now see in others that you avoid or run away from, believing they will have negative impact on you?

Which of the Light qualities on your list do you now see in others that leave you feeling inferior, inadequate, jealous or envious?

Which of those do you believe you could never proudly own?

Summary

Run over your highlighted list again, and ask yourself this – if you had to wear a T-shirt for an entire day with one of those traits printed on the front, which would be the most terrifying or leave you feeling the most embarrassed? T-shirts with slogans like, 'I am sexy', 'I am brilliant', 'I am gorgeous', 'I am powerful' 'I am arrogant', 'I am stupid' 'I am ugly' etc.

Light T-shirt slogan = *I am ...*

Dark T-shirt slogan = *I am ...*

EXERCISE 16:

Changing your Lenses

The intention behind this exercise is to change the way you perceive your Shadow Self. Search for a higher definition of each quality to seek resolve by putting it in a different context.

Start by redefining the confronting qualities you imagined on your T-shirts. If you are not sure about how to complete the exercise, refer to Maggie's example below.

Look at your list of Dark and Light Shadow traits. Now reinterpret the meaning you have attached to each of those traits until you are willing to claim them. It will help you to see those traits in a different context if you acknowledge some of your current strengths and are willing to trust them. That will allow you to balance the equation. e.g: If you are afraid to be stingy, trust the fact you can be generous and fair and accept you can also be mean. One doesn't cancel out the other!

Redefine your interpretation around your Dark Shadow qualities.

Redefine your interpretation around your Light Shadow qualities.

KEY COORDINATE NO. 11

In your journal, respond to the following in the separate section: Map of the Soul

What were three of the slogans on your Light Shadow T-shirts

Maggie's Example Exercise:

Dark Shadow:

SELFISH: When I am exhausted or don't genuinely feel as though it is in my best interests to do something I will say no – even if I appear to be selfish. I also know that I am generous, caring and loving and therefore I have nothing to

fear regarding selfishness.

VIOLENT: If someone broke in to my house and wanted to assault me, it would be in my best interests to protect myself. If that leads to me being violent then so be it. I am happy to claim this part of me knowing it has its place. I also recognize I am discerning, understanding and compassionate, therefore I am not afraid of being violent.

Light Shadow:

ASSERTIVE: If I voice my honest opinion and don't always agree with people, it doesn't mean that they won't love me. It means that they will have more respect for me. If I take action in my world and build a platform to proudly stand on, it doesn't mean that people will think I won't need them anymore. It also doesn't make me selfish or arrogant. I can be assertive and still let people support me and get close to me. If I am assertive and I make a mistake or hurt someone, I will trust that I am fair and considerate.

ADVENTUROUS: I can be adventurous and not feel disloyal. It doesn't mean I am abandoning others or disregarding their needs and preferences. If I am willing to also be ASSERTIVE, I can negotiate an amicable agreement and maintain my sense of responsibility. Not obligation or duty but responsibility. I can take action! I am even willing to make a fool of myself. I accept the fact that I may be seen as foolish and am willing to risk that. After all, being compliant at times is very foolish and that is what I have been – foolish!

MEDITATION

The intention behind this meditation is to make peace with your Dark Shadow and embrace more of your Light Shadow.

Find a comfortable position and begin to relax. Gently close your eyes.

Focus on your breathing and empty your mind of all thoughts. Take three deep breaths and exhale slowly.

Imagine yourself standing in the middle of a circle in a field. The sun is directly in front of you creating a shadow behind you.

Affirm to yourself, I am willing to claim both the light and dark parts of my nature – knowing I am an aspect of All That Is.

Turn around to face your Shadow. Look to the left, toward the Dark quadrant and allow images of the ominous, ugly, destructive parts of you to come into view. Pay particular attention to the qualities you know you have denied.

Connect with them energetically and just allow them to be as they are. Become aware of the density of their vibration and the way it makes you feel. View those aspects of you with compassion, knowing they are merely the parts of you that are estranged from love.

Now affirm:

'I accept all parts of my nature, knowing they have their place in creation. I simply let them be. I claim these parts of me and own them to honor my Soul.'

Turn your head to the right to face the quadrant of your Light Shadow. Allow images of the magnificent, brilliant, powerful, life-affirming aspects of you to come into view.

Pay particular attention to the qualities you know you have denied. Connect with them energetically and just allow them to be as they are.

Become aware of the radiance of their vibration and the way it makes you feel. View those parts of you with an open heart, knowing you have estranged them. Embrace them with your love.

Now affirm:

'I accept all parts of my nature, knowing they have their place in creation. I claim these parts of me and own them to honor my Soul.'

Once you have completed the ritual – take a deep breath and gently bring yourself out of the meditation.

Your checklist

1. Did you write in your journal on a regular basis to observe your thoughts and feelings?
2. Did you record any Soul-Speak?
3. Have you logged your insights, goals and aspirations?
4. Were you mindful of your intention?
5. Did you take time to contemplate the Divine Truth and the two Key Words?
6. Have you been using your **Pocket Affirmation** on a regular basis?
7. Have you taken the time to do your meditation to claim your Shadow?
8. Have you done your exercises and logged them?
9. Have you been conscious of identifying your Shadow by noticing who pushed your buttons or who you were in awe of?
10. If you haven't done any or all of these things then ask yourself - what stopped you?

You may be going into denial or avoidance around the topic for this particular level of self-discovery – what has your Ego been telling you? Those conversations reflect your limited beliefs about yourself. CHALLENGE THEM! Remember – your heart's desires are at stake.

LEVEL
7

During this level of the course you will explore your life's lessons and Soul Contracts to reach a deeper understanding of the journey of your Soul.

There are many things you are here to learn, but your primary life lesson is the most significant of all. It aligns with the subsequent lessons you elected to learn, weaving itself through the Dark and Light Matrix in your Soul's Hologram. By defining your life's lessons, you will gather clues to uncover your Soul's Purpose.

Claiming Autonomy and Freedom – Life Lessons

DIVINE TRUTH: You live in a world filled with love, abundance and joy. The way you perceive your world determines your experience.

KEY WORDS: Wisdom versus Ignorance

Wisdom springs from integrating the knowledge you gather in the world into your own personal experience. It brings illumination and an expansion of your awareness. Ignorance, by contrast, leaves you in the dark, denying your ability to search and stretch for deeper meaning and understanding, which leads to uncovering more of the truth.

'You are a magnificent being in the process of discovering more of your True Self. If you could perceive your life through the eyes of your Soul, you would see both the beginning and end of your journey and what lies beyond. You live into your Soul's unspoken agreements with the aim of learning your life's lessons.'

Many astrologers believe we choose our exact time of birth, according to the lessons our Soul needs to master to evolve to a higher level of consciousness. Your birth or Natal chart shows the positions of the stars at the time you were born at the location of your birth. Reading the data of your chart can offer you insight into your Soul's intention in regard to what you have chosen to learn in this life.

Although your Natal chart can serve as a useful tool to gain insight into your strengths, challenges and personality traits, what you do with those characteristics is determined by your free will. Whilst the position of the planets has an effect on your energy, every choice and decision you make steers the course of your destiny. Each of those choices is based on the way you perceive your life and the value you place on your intrinsic worth.

Entering the physical world you develop amnesia, losing sight of your true origin and full potential. Although you believe you are separate, you are never disconnected from the Source. Becoming enlightened pertains to ending that pretence and remembering who you are. Awakening the sleeping parts of your Soul is an integral part of your spiritual journey.

Although you are currently restricted by the limitations of your Ego;

beyond time and space the greater parts of you hold a much more expansive point of view. Your choices are far more liberal, encompassing the entirety of your Soul's Blueprint. From that heightened level of perception, you consider the beginning and end of the story and all of the possibilities in between.

Before you incarnate, you design a blueprint that includes a myriad of prospects to support your Soul's evolution. You chose your Divine Destiny, making certain you have everything you need to develop specific parts of your nature and master various lessons. You were born with particular gifts and talents that enable you to craft a life that allows you to be fully self-expressed. Your natural talents and strengths are there to be sharpened and honed into skills. They are there to be used as a means to help you overcome the specific challenges and shortcomings that you elected.

Reincarnation involves more than just a simple decision to undergo a physical lifetime. In the higher realms, between incarnations, many issues are considered. Keep in mind your incarnations do not manifest in linear fashion – they are all happening simultaneously. You are simply focusing on one aspect of your Soul's expression. It is more than likely that you have hundreds or thousands of incarnations in existence where your Soul is exploring the full range of its potential. Restricted by the boundaries of your Ego, it would be impossible for you to process all of that information, which is why you isolate lives and create semblance, bringing order to the chaos. You are following your own unique quest, shining a torch on various parts of your nature while you explore your multi-dimensional self.

Within each of your lifetimes there are common threads or themes where similar lessons are tackled. They could be considered as variations of one theme. It is not uncommon for a Soul to isolate certain characteristics in a given life and work on them almost exclusively. For example, if you are learning the value of compassion, your Soul may choose the physical vehicles of a nun, a doctor or the mother of a paraplegic child to master that characteristic.

In a number of incarnations you may have developed your intellectual prowess as a high priority, in which case studying the powers of your mind will be beneficial in certain ways, yet could be detrimental in others. You may choose to focus on your academic strength and intentionally disregard your emotions, casting parts of yourself into your Shadow. Through experiences in other lifetimes, you may focus primarily on your emotional development and purposefully underplay your intellectual capabilities to even the scales. You may also choose to progress at an easier pace, using a more balanced, steady method. In which case, you will keep different aspects of your personality developing at once, working through lessons more gradually, rather than in an intense, exaggerated way.

On a Soul level, you chose to be born with particular handicaps. When you made those choices, you knew you would naturally gravitate to develop other qualities to compensate. Those qualities indicate your primary focus for this lifetime. The strengths and weaknesses of your personality merely reflect your Soul's intention to stretch and grow. Developing your strengths enables you to attain self-mastery and transcend the Dark Matrix – a construct that you originally planned.

You selected the components of your Dark Matrix, which is made up of your limiting beliefs, attitudes, images, contracts and scripts. They establish the blockages and hurdles you set in place that give rise to your life's lessons. Like a cosmic blueprint, that information is hardwired in the patterns of your brain and within the chemistry of your body.

Your spiritual DNA offers you insight into your Soul's purpose. Whether you are here to master qualities such as loyalty, courage, authority, virtue or truth; by honoring the power and beauty of your Soul and Spirit, you automatically align with optimal or radiant futures. Those golden threads of opportunity are woven through the fabric of your Light Matrix and ultimately lead to a point of greatness.

Your life does have a higher purpose: you have chosen to incarnate into this particular body, at this particular time, for that specific reason. Whether you are conscious of that quest or asleep to your fortune, at certain points in your destiny, you are guided by your Soul to overcome your weaknesses and establish a sense of balance and harmony. They are the Destiny Points on the Map of your Soul that you chose before your birth.

Those milestones flag periods of exponential growth where your talents, strengths and gifts are fortified. During those defining moments, both negative and positive, parts of you recede while others spring to life. Because you have free will, the final outcome of those defining moments always depends on you. The way you approach those challenges will indicate your level of progress – moving closer to or further away from love, joy, individuality and freedom.

By being responsible, and enjoying the power that responsibility brings, you will accelerate your growth. The one key thing to monitor is your feelings of not deserving. That notion filters through your thoughts, feelings, attitudes and beliefs, which weakens your choices. This is why your journey of self-discovery needs to encompass acknowledging your blockages along with fostering and utilizing your capabilities.

Defining moments are often Destiny Points where Soul Contracts begin. You encounter emissaries for your Soul that appear to play out a particular role, which is mutually agreed on in the higher realms. There is always an equal exchange in the universe. No matter what you choose to play out – both parties benefit from a higher perspective. Those contracts are created before you were born but they are never fixed. They continue to manifest during the course of your evolution and we discussed them in more detail in Level 6.

We are all here to support one another on a Soul level. That is why it is incredibly important you remain humble and stay open to being loved, acknowledged and supported. Your Soul will work through others to deliver the gifts that life has to offer you. Agreements are made and a meeting is orchestrated using the law of synchronicity. The contracts are then activated according to your freewill.

The Soul Contracts you put in place comprise of a multitude of options. They include exchanges that are sealed with love and delivered with sheer grace. Energetically, we are all part of the unified field – communicating on a unconscious level. The potential players in your world register what you send out through the unspoken word. This is how the contracts for your relationships are formed.

In each of those relationships, you have the potential to grow through love and joy. That old cliché 'no pain, no gain' is a gross misconception. Love is the most powerful energy that exists in the universe – it above all helps us to heal and grow. Whenever you are genuinely willing to experience a new way of relating, and open up to being loved, you send out an invitation to both existing and potential players, altering the conditions in your contracts.

Your Soul's Blueprint includes alternatives that allow you to be fully self-expressed with complementary counterparts. Within the framework of that blueprint there are a myriad of future possibilities and potential Soul contacts. Not one but many.

You have a multitude of wonderful alternatives in the offering that you are free to choose from. Amongst those connections, you have longstanding relationships with your Soul family – a group of beings who you collaborate with over the course of lifetimes, and in between, to support one another in your growth. Prior to incarnating, you set up agreements on how to help one another learn your life's lessons, often taking on similar challenges. Your Soul family, who are a part of your 'inner circle', are a group of kindred spirits on the path. Often they show up during defining moments to inspire or help implement change.

When you meet a member of your Soul family or important teacher, there is usually an instant recognition and you quickly form a deep connection. There is often a sense you have known each other before. Based on the fact that we communicate with one another beyond time and space, especially in the dream state, this isn't too surprising. There is usually a distinct quality that you recognize about the person that stands out like a beacon. Whether it is their eyes, their laugh or even a small idiosyncrasy around the way they dress, something about the person progressively draws you to them. Beyond those little features, we each have a unique energetic signature, which endorses our Soul's Blueprint.

There are also Souls in outer circles, who you agree to connect with over a series of lifetimes, who play significant roles. You make contractual agreements that set the stage for your mutual growth. Often these arrangements involve Souls you have been associated with over hundreds of lifetimes.

If you are unwilling to take advantage of opportunities to grow in a particular life, you will often do so when you pass over. It is always your choice. Between incarnations there is a period of contemplation and searching for deeper understanding. Every aspect of a life is examined and reviewed to bring greater awareness. There is nothing outside of yourself that will force you to look at your issues or face them. You have free will in the physical world and other dimensions; your fundamental beliefs determine what you create in this world and beyond.

What you think and feel each day will become the fabric of your next existence. You are setting the stage for your next life now. There are no magic mantras or fairy wands that will make you wise. The only way you will expand your consciousness is by deepening your level of compassion and understanding – of yourself and others. Your everyday experiences and beliefs contain the answers; they hold the key to your liberation.

In each of your lifetimes you attract the features that you place most of your attention on. If you vividly focus on the injustices that have been done to you, then you attract more of the experience to find a point of resolve. Similarly, any successes you have achieved in this life, and any abilities you have developed, you have worked out through past experiences and stretching your beliefs. They are rightfully yours to claim based on your intrinsic power to create. If you look at the people you closely associate with in this world, you will gauge what kind of person you are. You are drawn to each through basic similarities and common beliefs.

Your biological family and genetic heritage is the bond you accepted. That original foundation gives rise to your most significant life's lessons. Within that exchange you receive your legacy of love, which you are here to expand on. It sets the dimensions of love and your capacity to give and receive; highlighting the conditions you are here to dismantle.

Everyone feels a lack of deserving to some degree. It is part of the human condition. Breaking that vicious cycle is one of our collective lessons; along with learning to consciously create success by confidently trusting our inner and outer resources.

We are all here to master one significant quality that has the potential to set us free from the mire. If you consider each of the Noble Merits below, associated with the Knights of the Round Table, they will serve to indicate which particular strength will aid you in your individual quest of fulfilling your Soul's purpose. Utilizing that asset will help you transcend your Dark Matrix and move toward greatness.

The Twelve Noble Merits:

Honor – respect and integrity
Gallantry – attentiveness and thoughtfulness
Courage – bravery, valor and daring
Courtesy – kindness and consideration
Loyalty – faithfulness and allegiance
Virtue – goodness and morality
Authority – power and mastery
Truth – honesty and authenticity
Generosity – goodwill and benevolence
Service – care and support
Humility – modesty and innocence
Nobility – pride and dignity

No matter what our personality projects, beneath that façade we are complex beings with many layers to our nature. If we were able view one another on a multi-dimensional level, considering the diversity of our lifetimes, we would be far more generous in the way we perceive one another and be less likely to judge. No matter what we have done in the past, we have the ability to change by claiming more of our goodness, truth, power and beauty.

During my sessions, uncovering a person's life's lessons has helped them to understand the whys and wherefores beneath the living drama of their existence. Presenting them with the bigger picture made it easier for them to realize they had the capacity to change, regardless of their circumstances. This was the case with one woman who walked through the door extremely composed; yet underneath she was emotionally torn.

Laura was strikingly beautiful and tastefully groomed in a well-tailored business suit. When she boldly announced we had less than ninety minutes, I knew she had no idea how deep we were about to go.

Entering the silence, I talked to her about a series of significant lifetimes where she had repeated the same pattern in her relationships. In one of those incarnations in Europe, she had nursed and supported her gravely ill husband. Withholding her fears, and suppressing her anguish, she efficiently maintained their financial affairs and cared for their children. Helplessly watching her husband slowly wasting away, she begged him not to give up. When he finally passed away, his death fortified her misleading core belief that her love wasn't powerful enough to sustain the things she loved. I could see her current viewpoint was perpetuating the same karmic influences. To change her fate she needed to alter her views around partnership.

Stunned by my words, she turned pale and stared blankly into space. After taking a deep breath, she announced her husband had cancer and that she was reliving precisely the same circumstances. Although she attended to his every need, she was annoyed that he wouldn't seek alternative methods of treatment and continually shut her out. Locked in an isolated world of depression, he refused to communicate or respond to her tenderness. He shunned her love in favor of harboring his resentment, loathing the fact he had the disease.

Although Laura was overtaxed, fearful and lonely, she swallowed her pain. To spare her husband from further angst, she refused to shed a single tear or utter a word of complaint.

It was clear from Laura's session that she was reliving a similar scenario in this life to garner a valuable lesson on the power of her love and her capacity to make a difference. Her husband was merely responding to her core belief that unless she was strong, productive and resourceful, her contribution was worthless. The softer, gentler sides of her nature were deemed redundant, particularly in the face of adversity. The healer and muse within Laura were cast off into the Shadow, overpowered by the administrator. Mirroring her own thoughts, her husband lived into the script she formulated as a child.

When Laura was eight, her father left, leaving her mother to raise Laura and her two brothers. Part of Laura's contract with both parents was to always be independent and responsible by taking care of her two smaller brothers, one of whom had asthma. Laura equated having fun with being selfish and aligned freedom with disloyalty. Her attitude was fostered by the tag line her mother repeatedly used when berating her absent father. She referred to him as a 'good-for-nothing', who preferred to be footloose and fancy-free rather than take care of his family.

Laura's legacy of love supported the theory that love equals sacrifice and being of service. Her primary lesson was to redefine love to include – trust, security and pleasure. She had played the role of martyr over many life times, relinquishing her happiness to be seen as noble. Once again she had forfeited her personal dreams in order to attend to needs of others, equating love with obligation and duty.

Laura's Soul was compelling her to examine the virtue of loyalty – not only to others but also to herself. Unless both partners are willing to respond to the love that exists in the relationship, and be responsible for keeping it alive, it will diminish. Both Laura and her husband shut down parts of themselves, which cast a Dark Shadow over their union.

In her incarnation in Europe and her current lifetime, Laura had blamed both of her husbands for putting an end to her dreams. After discussing the issue in her session, she realized that although she had accused both husbands of emotionally deserting her, from a higher perspective she had been disloyal to herself. Both realities were a reflection of her core belief that she didn't deserve to have fun.

For Laura suffering in silence was no longer an option; she was tired of forfeiting her own happiness to support her husband's sense of despair. Her sullenness was affecting their six-year-old daughter and so the cost had become too great. She could see that tiptoeing around her husband for almost two years had been a mistake; joy and gratitude would have been the perfect medicine for both of them.

Charting your course

Write your intention in your journal. Because you will be working specifically with your life's lessons, use a declaration that aligns with claiming your autonomy and freedom.

Perhaps it is something like:

> **'During this level of the course I intend to be mindful of what I need to learn from certain situations and notice how often that same lesson continues to present itself.'**

Or you may prefer something more direct like:

> **'As I progress through this level of the course I intend to shift my perception to recognize that I live in an abundant world that I create.'**

Or

> **'I intend to be mindful of the fact that I am here in this world to consciously create success by recognizing that I am whole and complete.'**

Choose statements that you are genuinely willing to abide by. Make your declaration of intent in the presence of your Higher Self and Soul, so you know you will make every effort to stand by your word.

Write this **Pocket Affirmation** *in your journal and post it in a prominent position to refer to as your daily mantra.*

**'I live in a world filled with love, abundance and joy.
I now claim my autonomy and freedom, knowing
I deserve to have fun.'**

Write the Key Words **Wisdom versus Ignorance** *in your journal and contemplate them on a daily basis. Become conscious of which of the two you align with more often, to help you assess where you give your power away.*

Do the meditation for this level for a minimum of 15 minutes at least three times before moving onto the next level. You may want to record any insights in your journal.

The process

The first step to uncovering your life's lessons is to pay attention to the repetitive patterns that occur in your life. They hold the key to unraveling the mystery of what parts of your nature you are here to claim and which specific talents you have chosen to nurture and enjoy. Your defining moments will serve to offer you clues along with your scripts and psychic contracts.

The destiny points on the Map of the Soul will also highlight the Soul Contracts you put in place to help foster your individual strengths and build your confidence. Stringing together those vital points will steer you towards your Soul's purpose.

In the process of defining your lessons, one will stand out as being paramount. That primary lesson will specifically relate to one area, such as claiming your power, mastering your Ego or recognizing the majesty of love. Search for clues by pulling back from your reality and become the Objective Observer.

As an example: if honoring your emotions is a significant lesson for you on a Soul level, you would have set the stage to play that out. Perhaps you were born into a family where expressing emotions was discouraged and the depth of feeling was therefore unfamiliar to you. By starting out with that as a handicap, and moving on to develop that strength independently, you would be apt to honor the depth of your emotions through freewill and conscious choice, claiming that attribute in the name of your Soul – re-instating your authority.

Keep in mind that whatever your life's lessons are, you initially elected them. As difficult as you think those tests or trials may be, there is no such thing as 'bad karma' – you are not paying penance or seeking retribution. Because you chose your lessons, you can change them. You are here to instigate balance and harmony within yourself, which is then reflected in your relationships and mirrored back in the illusion of the physical world.

Write your answers to the following exercises in your journal.

EXERCISE 16:
Finding the Clues in your Life Script

Your family and genetic heritage is the bond which gives rise to your most significant life's lessons. It also designates your legacy of love, which you are here to expand on. By closely reviewing your silent contracts and life scripts, you can determine your capacity to give and receive. Your life script also emphasizes the limitations you are here to overcome.

The intention of the following exercise is to determine which of your parents' philosophies and behaviors you endorsed to create the springboard for your growth. Your aim is to string together the clues that point to your life's lessons.

Before you begin, go back and read the life script you wrote in Level 5 to help you answer the following questions.

What strengths have you developed as a result of your experiences?

What key qualities did you need to claim from your Light Shadow after defining your script?

What was the greatest challenge that appeared for you as the main character in your life script?

Reading through the list of the Twelve Noble Merits, if you were to choose one that would liberate you as the main character in your life script, which one would it be?

The Twelve Noble Merits

Honor – respect and integrity
Gallantry – attentiveness and thoughtfulness
Courage – bravery, valor and daring
Courtesy – kindness and consideration
Loyalty – faithfulness and allegiance
Virtue – goodness and morality
Authority – power and mastery
Truth – honesty and authenticity
Generosity – goodwill and benevolence
Service – care and support
Humility – modesty and innocence
Nobility – pride and dignity

Reviewing your answers to the previous questions, what do you think your life's lessons are?

KEY COORDINATE NO. 12

In your journal, respond to the following in the separate section: Map of the Soul

Which of the Twelve Noble Merits are you here to claim?

Laura's Completed Example:

Based on my life script, I have developed the following strengths – I am loyal, disciplined, creative, intelligent, inventive, brave and optimistic. I care deeply about others and strive to support them. I have had to use those strengths to build the foundation of my life.

I needed to claim being fun, adventurous, sensual, sexy and beautiful from my Light Shadow

My greatest challenge in my life script was to give up being a martyr and stop considering other people's needs before my own. Along with breaking the habit of denying myself pleasure and my right to have fun.

*The Noble Merit that can liberate me in my life script is – **Nobility** – pride and dignity*

My life's lessons are – to know my worth by claiming my pride and dignity. My primary lesson is about love – specifically acknowledging the power of my love. My hurdle has been to learn how to honor others and myself equally... Etc.

EXERCISE 17 – PART A:

Tracing your Biological Threads

The aim of the following exercise is to locate the areas where you have shifted beyond your biological legacy and used your individual merits to grow. It will give you an indication of where you have claimed your Soul's legacy and highlight the strengths you chose to master your life's lessons.

Fill out the answers for your mother first and then repeat the exercise for your father. If your primary guardians weren't your biological parents, complete the exercise using their names.

Write a very brief synopsis that encapsulates your mother's life script by filing out the blank spaces below:

My mother played out the role of _____ in her life. When
she did, she exhibited the following strengths and weaknesses
_____. Because she chose that path, she never achieved
the following _____.

Now change the ending of her script, by imagining she had an epiphany somewhere along the line and completely knew her worth. She then went on to be totally self-expressed and fulfill her dreams. With this new information answer the following questions:

1. What specific strengths would your mother have needed to develop to change her position? e.g. creativity, intelligence, uniqueness, courage, compassion, etc.
2. What characteristics would she have needed to transcend? e.g. victimhood, martyrdom, self-pity, arrogance, righteousness, submissiveness, etc.
3. What would she have had to be willing to do? E.g. Been honest, responsible for her impact, claimed her talent, stop putting everyone first, etc.
4. Repeat both parts of the exercise substituting your father or alternate guardian.

Laura's Completed Exercise:

My mother played out the role of *stoic caretaker* in her life. When she did, she exhibited the following strengths and weaknesses – she was *loyal, hardworking, devoted and selfless. She was also rigid, sorrowful and pessimistic, denying her right to a joyful life.* Because she chose that path, she never achieved the following – *having a loyal husband, being fully appreciated by her husband, being creatively self-expressed, establishing a significant career, traveling and exploring the world, and developing her intellect.*

1. The strengths my mother needed to develop to change her position were: *creativity, intelligence, inventiveness, adventurousness, courage, optimism, and playfulness.*
2. The characteristics she needed to transcend were: *victimhood, martyrdom, self-pity, rigidity, blame, criticism, pessimism and tedium.*
3. She would have had to be willing to: *embrace change, be open to being supported and loved, trust men to be there for her, recognize her beauty and claim her talent as a resourceful planner and strategist regarding business affairs.*

4. My father played out the role of *carefree playboy* in his life. When he did, he exhibited the following strengths and weaknesses – he was *fun loving, playful, charismatic, popular, adventurous and a risk taker. He was also indulgent, self-centered, irresponsible and dishonest.* Because he chose that path, he never achieved the following – *establishing security, being honored and respected by others, sticking to things long term and having close intimate relationships.*

5. The strengths my father needed to develop to change his position were: *being loyal, committed, responsible and responsive, kind, tender, open and honest.*

6. The characteristics he needed to transcend were: *destructiveness, recklessness, thoughtlessness and disloyalty.*

7. He would have had to be willing to: *be grateful, humble and loving, considering the feelings of others as well as his own. He would have had to recognize that he was genuinely loved.*

EXERCISE 17 – PART B:
Finding the Gold in Your Biological Threads

To complete this exercise, review what you have just written about each of your parents and answer the following questions.

Your aim is to locate which threads in their life you have successfully moved beyond and where you still need to focus your attention and grow. Clues to some of your life's lessons are woven through the answers.

Looking at the synopsis of your mother's life script, pay particular attention to the list of things she didn't achieve. Run through the list and make a note of which of those things you have personally achieved and those you haven't.

Have you developed the specific strengths your mother needed to develop to change her position? Make a note of which of those strengths you have and which you haven't developed.

What have you achieved that your mother didn't? What have you yet to achieve?

Look at the characteristics she needed to transcend. Which of those traits have you overcome and which are you yet to overcome?

Look at the things she needed to do. Which of those have you done and which remain on your list?

Run through the Noble Merits and choose one that would have liberated your mother in her script. Have you claimed that merit personally?

Repeat the exercise with your father or alternate guardian.

Reviewing your answers to the previous questions, which of your life's lessons do you think you have already mastered and which still remain? Of those, which do you think is your primary life lesson?

KEY COORDINATE NO. 13

In your journal, respond to the following in the separate section: Map of the Soul

Which of your life's lessons do you think is your primary life lesson?

Laura's Completed Example:
My Mother –

The strengths I have developed that my mother needed to develop to change her position are:
My creativity, intelligence, inventiveness, courage and optimism.
The strengths I haven't developed are:
I am not adventurous and playful.
The things I haven't yet achieved:
I haven't travelled and explored the world. I am not fully appreciated by my husband.

The things I have achieved that my **mother** didn't:

I have a loyal husband, I am creatively self-expressed, I have established a significant career and developed my intellect.

The traits I have overcome are:

Victimhood, self-pity, criticism and pessimism

The traits I am yet to overcome are :

Martyrdom, rigidity, blame and tedium.

The things my mother needed to do that I have done are:

I have been supported and loved. I have claimed my talent as a resourceful planner and strategist regarding business affairs.

The ones that remain on my list are:

I need to trust men to be there for me. I also need to recognize my beauty.

The Noble Merit my mother needed to claim was:

Courage *– bravery, valor and daring. Yes, I have claimed that noble merit!*

My Father –

The strengths I have developed that my father needed to develop to change his position are:

I am loyal, committed, responsible and responsive, kind, tender,

The strengths I haven't developed are:

Openess and honesty.

The things I haven't yet achieved:

I haven't had close, tender, intimate relationships.

The things I have achieved that my **father** didn't:

I have established security. I am honored and respected by others. I stick to things long term.

The traits I have overcome are:

I am no longer destructive, reckless, thoughtless or disloyal.

The traits I am yet to overcome are:

N.A.

The things my father needed to do that I have done are:

I am humble and loving, I am grateful, I do consider the feelings of others.

The ones that remain on my list are:

I still need to consider my own feelings while I remain sensitive to other people's feelings. I also need to realize that I am genuinely loved.

The Noble Merit my father needed to claim was:

Virtue *– goodness and morality. Yes, I have claimed that noble merit!*

My life's lessons have been to:

Be loyal to myself as well as others and speak my truth. To strive towards creating equality in my relationships. To use the noble merits of Courage and Virtue! To claim the noble merit of Nobility. To learn to have fun.

EXERCISE 18 – PART A:

Pinpointing your Destiny Points – Childhood.

The intention behind this exercise is to find the events in your childhood, between the ages of four to ten, where you experienced intense positive emotions such as love, joy, passion, enthusiasm and freedom. You may have also felt hope, trust and optimism as you looked toward a promising future. Then ask yourself what decision you made about yourself, e.g. I am brave, I am artistic, I am loved etc.

Cast your thoughts and feelings back to your childhood and allow memories to drift through your mind. You may find an unexpected event pops up out of the blue. If you find it difficult to remember your childhood, think about the things you liked to do. Once you open that file in your subconscious the information should just come to you.

Write a short synopsis of the story that describes one or two of your most significant defining moments.

1. I remember when I was _____ years of age, I felt excited when (event) _

    _____

    _____.

2. When that happened, I felt confident because _____

    _____ and I specifically felt (e.g. loved, honored etc)_____

    _____. The outcome was that I saw myself as___

    _____.

I knew from that day on that I could always trust my following strengths:

_____.

3. Aside from my parents, the following people stand out as helping me and supporting me through that process: _____

_____.

Laura's Completed Exercise:

1. I remember when I was *Nine* years of age, I felt excited when *I won two medals for swimming when I represented the State.*

2. When that happened, I felt confident because *everyone congratulated me for my strength and dedication* and I specifically felt *honored, inspired and optimistic.* The outcome was that I saw myself as *a winner in life.* I knew from that day on that I could always trust my following strengths: *my stamina, resilience, discipline, and I knew I was capable of achieving what I wanted when I strived to win.*

3. Aside from my parents, the following people stand out as helping me and supporting me through that process: *My swimming coach Ron – he taught me never to give up. My best friend Celia who taught me the value of loyalty.*

EXERCISE 18 – PART B:

Pinpointing your Destiny Points – Adolescence

Repeat the same exercise in relationship to your teenage years. Your aim is to find at least one incident between the ages of eleven and eighteen, where you experienced intense passion and joy. This will pinpoint one or more of your positive defining moments and Soul Contracts.

Write a short synopsis of the story that describes the most significant defining moment when you were a teenager.

1. I remember when I was _____years of age, I felt excited when (*event*): __

_____

_____.

2. When that happened, I felt confident because _____
   and I specifically felt: (*e.g. loved, honored etc*) _____
   The outcome was I saw myself as_____
   _____. I knew from that day on that I could always
   trust my following strengths: _____
   _____.

3. Aside from my parents, the following people stand out as helping me and
   supporting me through that process: _____
   _____.

4. Write one sentence that describes and summarizes the positive defining
   moment from your childhood.

   _____

   _____

5. Write one sentence that describes and summarizes the positive defining
   moment from your teenage years.

   _____

   _____

Laura's Completed Exercise:

1. I remember when I was sixteen years of age, I felt excited when *I wrote a
   short story and it was published in the school magazine and then the local
   paper.*

2. When that happened, I felt confident because *I saw I had talent as a writer*
   and I specifically felt *honored, proud, alive, joyful and passionate about my
   creativity.* The outcome was I saw myself as *creative, unique, talented and
   successful.* I knew from that day on that I could always trust my following
   strengths: *my creativity, ingenuity and intellect.*

3. Aside from my parents, the following people stand out as helping me and
   supporting me through that process: *my English teacher Mrs Spaulding
   who taught me about the value of not being afraid to let my imagination come
   to life. She was instrumental in helping me believe I had the talent to really
   stand out.*

4. The sentence that describes and summarizes the defining moment from my childhood. *When I won two gold medals for swimming.*
5. The sentence that describes and summarizes the defining moment from my teenage years. *When my short story was published when I was sixteen.*

MEDITATION

The intention behind this meditation is help you ground the Noble Merit that you are here to claim. Once you take on more of that attribute, you will embrace your power to heal and transform your life.

Find a comfortable position and begin to relax. Gently close your eyes.

Focus on your breathing and empty your mind of all thoughts. Take three deep breaths and exhale slowly.

Allow your imagination to expand and cast your thoughts back to one positive defining moment from your childhood.

Engage with all of your senses. Feel the joy, freedom and aliveness that the situation brings.

Now focus on the Noble Merit you are here to claim and align with the energy of that quality.

Feel it fully and affirm:

'I claim the merit of _____ knowing my true worth.'

Move forward in time to the positive defining moment from your teenage years. Engage with all of your senses. Feel the joy, freedom and aliveness that the situation brings.

Now focus on the Noble Merit you are here to claim and align with the energy of that quality. Feel it fully and affirm:

'I claim the merit of _____ knowing my true worth.'

Imagine placing a cloak around your shoulders that represents the Noble Merit you have identified. Feel the energy of the quality and declare:

'I wear the mantle of _____aligning with my true destiny.'

Allow the cloak to become invisible. Sense it as an energy field of light that surrounds you.

Once you have completed the ritual – take a deep breath and gently bring yourself out of the meditation.

Note: To build your confidence, sense the invisible cloak of energy surrounding you at times whenever you need to use that strength. It will also help to use the accompanying affirmation:

'I claim the merit of _____ knowing my true worth.'

Your checklist

1. Did you write in your journal on a regular basis to observe your thoughts and feelings?
2. Did you record any Soul-Speak?
3. Have you logged your insights, goals and aspirations?
4. Were you mindful of your intention?
5. Did you take time to contemplate the Divine Truth and the two Key Words?
6. Have you been using your **Pocket Affirmation** on a regular basis?
7. Have you taken time to meditate for a minimum of 15 minutes on at least three occasions?
8. Have you done your exercises and logged them?
9. Have you been conscious of your Noble Merit and willing to claim it to support your Heart's Desire?
10. If you haven't done any or all of these things then ask yourself – what stopped you?

You may be going into denial or avoidance around the topic for this particular level of self-discovery – what has your Ego been telling you? Those conversations reflect your limited beliefs about yourself. CHALLENGE THEM! Remember – your heart's desires are at stake.

LEVEL

8

During this level of the course you will learn to identify your Authentic Self. You will begin to feel free to be the person you genuinely want to be and create a life that you love. Your Soul is there to guide you every step of the way as you move gracefully toward fulfilling your true destiny. You will be steered toward honoring your preferences rather than being curtailed by other people's forecasts and options. As an adult you don't need permission to follow your dreams or require someone else to determine your course. Your intention during this level of the course is to focus your attention on the things you like to do, and follow the call of your heart.

Following True North – Authentic Self

DIVINE TRUTH: What you receive is based on what you are willing to have and not on what you deserve.

KEY WORDS: Authenticity versus Self-Consciousness

Being authentic is an essential step to discovering your True Self. It allows you to place your Ego aside and follow your heart. Self-consciousness will close you down to being acknowledged, supported and loved, robbing you of your freedom.

'Your deepest feelings are the gauge which indicates if you are following your intuition and aligning with True North. If you are moving in a positive direction in life your emotions will be buoyant. If you steer off-course your feelings become constricted.'

The compass is a universal symbol of direction and navigation. Following True North is about making your pathway through life easier and more fulfilling. It is based on tapping into your unique gifts and talents and expressing them freely. Entering that receptive state means celebrating your creativity, allowing your knowledge and wisdom to blossom. In this way you live with aliveness and vitality, knowing your true worth.

Aliveness relates to the depth and quality of what you experience as well as how much you achieve. It aligns with love, trust, enthusiasm and expectancy, or excited anticipation. As you take steps toward truly loving yourself, and sharing that love with others, you become more alive. Being authentic is the key, embracing your full range of emotions as you seek the joy of living a spirited, Soul-ful life.

Over the course of your life you have felt every conceivable emotion. Each emotion either gravitates toward love or fear. By recognizing the power of love, you can accept all parts of your nature without trepidation and authentically choose who you want to be.

If on the other hand you refuse to claim your light, and deny your brilliance, you will move away from the source of life and away from love. Operating from the lowest parts of your consciousness you align with emotions such as envy, jealousy, rage, blame, hate, violence, cruelty, hopelessness and despair. Those, and other constrictive emotions, gravitate towards the denser quadrant in the unified field, giving rise to the destructive sides of your nature. If you enter into those states, you have merely withdrawn from love, straying away from your True Self.

In a state of love, you take action from a place of love. In a state of fear you move towards struggle and control. Your Authentic Self aligns with love and not with fear. That is why it is imperative you monitor your feelings and are committed to being true to yourself, rather than seeking outside approval. You are the one who ultimately assesses if you are good enough to be loved. What you receive is based on what you are willing to have and not on what you deserve. Balance, flexibility and humility are the keys to being authentic. And it is your Authentic Self that will point you towards True North.

To remain true to yourself it is essential that you stay in touch with your feelings. To create anything solely out of sheer will and determination will eventually leave you dissatisfied or uninspired. You can use the power of your will to drive you forward and yet, if you overlook the call of your heart, it will be an empty endeavor.

The same emptiness will occur if you consistently operate from duty or obligation, rather than considering your personal preferences. If this is the case, you need to look deeper within yourself to sense more of your Soul, rather than lean heavily on conformity, logic or reason.

It is very important that you are clear on where your priorities lie and how much time and energy you devote to certain situations. Remember – where your attention goes your energy follows. Your self-esteem depends on being flexible with your identity, exploring and expressing more of your True Self. If you become too attached to upholding your identity you will become self-conscious. This is a telltale sign your Ego is running the show, which is the direct opposite of authentic self-expression. Therefore being self-conscious is a clear indication that you have disengaged from your Authentic Self. That poses one important question: Who are you living your life for?

You have the opportunity and the power to create any identity that you choose. It is simply a matter of honoring your preferences and recognizing that you have the full spectrum of human qualities within you. That means giving up any debilitating conversations that have driven you in the past, that distort your self-image. It is important that you claim your power and value your essence, by refusing to surrender to negativity. That step will take you closer to knowing your Soul and acknowledging your Spirit in a deep and rewarding way.

If you are primarily focused on monitoring your level of performance or appearance you will align with Ego. By contrast, if you stay fully present in the moment, you can remain humble and graciously receptive. You sense how to respond to what is going on in your world rather than being concerned about other people's opinions. Your creative energy can then flow through you and your imagination can become a powerful resource to use to gather insight and information. The key is to give yourself permission to be all that you can be – without being inhibited or restricted by others. After all, you are the guardian of your Soul and the caretaker of your own heart. Unless you give yourself a wide birth for self-expression parts of you will remain in the Shadow.

Living your life based on avoiding disappointment, criticism or failure will quickly douse your passion and confine you to a life of mediocrity. If you are hindered by fear or reticence, look to see where you are projecting your past into the future and shift your focus – otherwise you will continue to feed your negative expectations.

Following your Soul's call to adventure moves you forward into expansion. It takes courage and a commitment to discover more of your True Self, which is why it is vitally important you disengage from Ego. Listening to the Ego's prattle will drown out the voice of your heart and keep you playing small. If you are unsure of what you really want to do, or which direction to take, it is wise to search a little deeper for the answers. Look at your resistance to following your heart or viewing your full potential. Fear and doubt will always cause confusion, restricting your view of what is genuinely possible.

Regarding your happiness as a genuine priority is an act that indicates you are willing to grow and give up your attachment to the past. That means focusing your attention on what brings you joy, which will steer you toward a range of optimal futures and set you on the path of graceful creation. That course of True North enables you to achieve the maximum benefits with a minimum expenditure of energy.

When you give up control and surrender to the flow of life, moving into 'the zone' – the energy stream of love, joy, individuality and freedom is released. Once you align with that resonance, you attract synchronistic events that enable you to swiftly progress.

If your passion or interest is sparked in any one area, then this is a definite clue to which path to take. Passion emerges from your heart and aligns you with love and joy. Anything you create from that expansive state will immediately bring you in touch with your Soul and produce the greatest rewards. When you naturally gravitate towards things that inspire your curiosity, and fuel your desire to learn and experience more, you are right on track.

Your inherent talents are vitally important. They are precious gifts that can be used to craft a wonderful life that denotes your unique signature. Consider them carefully rather than take them for granted; they deserve to be cherished. Whether you are a gifted artist, musician, cook, gardener, caretaker, inventor, strategist, teacher, healer or performer – nurture your talents and use them. Don't give your Ego permission to interpret their value. Out of respect for your Soul, choose to honor your merits and acknowledge them as part of your Essence.

Creativity does not solely apply to artistic expression. It relates to your ability to create meaningful new ideas, forms, methods or interpretations. When any creative pursuit absorbs your attention to such a degree that you are 'lost in the moment', you move beyond your identity to engage with your Soul and Spirit – operating in the heart of the zone. Your structured identity disappears and you presence more of your True Self. You are directly in touch with your Authentic-Self, allowing your Soul to express itself freely through you. At which point, the following paradox applies – 'it is about you and it is not about you'. Embracing your attributes to that degree will bring you in touch with your unique genius.

Genius does not necessarily apply to having a high IQ or being perfect. You were born with the seed of genius. It is there to cultivate using wisdom, patience, and your capacity to know with persistence and the willingness to be wrong in the pursuit of what is right, beautiful or true. Your genius awakens through dreaming and visioning, by shifting your perspective of what is possible. It exists within you and is the substance from which miracles occur. A miracle is simply something more than you expect, which produces wonder and awe. This is the ultimate place to be in all situations – a state of complete innocence.

If you allow yourself to be grateful throughout the creative process, your progress can be exponential. As you start feeling grateful for what you have, you start having more things to feel grateful for. You have to be willing to hold a positive view of your capabilities and be open to taking action.

Your internal resources provide you with everything you need to create a life that you love. Selecting a path that challenges your skills is an essential component in making valuable choices, along with your willingness to grow and learn. You will never be fully prepared for everything you face in life, which is why it is important to strengthen your ability to trust yourself.

When you face big decisions and choices, trust can become an issue that hinders your progress. Rather than jumping into the deep end, it can be beneficial to run through the list of pros and cons. It is wise to gather as much information as you can on where to base your trust, so you feel confident taking action. The best way to run through the process is to gather information from your mind, body, feelings and intuition and look at the combined data.

Become aware of your body's muscular and nerve responses to see if you are tense or relaxed. Get in touch with your feelings and watch what emotions come to the surface. Call on your intuition and sense your instinctive responses. You may then want to make a list of the advantages and disadvantages to speculate and make a deduction. Watch for your gut level responses and hunches. Once you have connected with all aspects of you, the trust will emerge.

Your Authentic Self versus your Sub-personalities

Once you are aligned with True North, make sure you are clear on which part of you is in the driver's seat so you stay on course. You have developed certain behavior patterns over the course of your life to get you what you want and keep you safe. There are different aspects of your personality that come into play at certain times and they are not all productive. They are like sub-personalities that emerge when you feel anxious or shift into 'control mode'. Fueled by Ego, they can sabotage your progress, lead you astray or create conflict. So be very conscious of which part of you is motivating your thoughts, feelings and expectations and driving you into the future.

To maintain your connection with your Authentic Self, you need to keep your sub-personalities in the back seat and stay awake at the wheel. Identifying and naming your sub-personalities will help you be on the ball. After awhile, you will instinctively sense where you are coming from and shift gears automatically.

While working with clients, I noticed by naming their sub-personalities it helped them to pinpoint when their negative beliefs came into play and triggered constricting emotions. They were able to see that instead of claiming the virtues of their Authentic Self, they chose a lesser role, manipulating or controlling their reality rather than consciously creating from a place of integrity. As an example, when Barbara came to see me she had two sub-personalities which she needed to identify and master. *Bashful* Barbara, who continually deflected her power of authority, was hypersensitive and always wanted to withdraw. When that particular aspect of Barbara took the driver's seat, she did a u-turn in life and retracted her energy from projects, giving up or wanting to hide or hibernate. By contrast, *Brazen* Barbara was intense, direct and extremely willful, bulldozing anyone who got in her way. She swung the pendulum from one extreme to the other, attempting to find balance.

When Barbara was in touch with her Authentic Self, she was highly creative, witty and loving. Her Ego took a back seat, allowing the receptive and assertive sides of her nature to come into balance. She was a powerful, productive and incredibly passionate young woman who achieved great results. We named her Authentic Self *Buoyant* Barbara. When Barbara stepped into those shoes, she was glowing and radiant – a magnet for opportunities.

Confusion and doubt were the two elements that triggered her sub-personalities to surface. She would then withdraw (Bashful Barbara) or defend and attack (with Brazen Barbara in control).

To stay on track, Barbara needed to watch for contradictory ideas or conversations that ran through her thoughts and quickly nip them in the bud, otherwise she would veer off the path and lose sight of her True Self. The same applied when she projected her past disappointments into the future, diminishing her expectations.

Barbara eventually got to a point where her Authentic Self came to the forefront to such a degree that she completely altered her life. She successfully built a new identity based on who she authentically wanted to be rather than what she feared. She worked with her sub-personalities to integrate their qualities and transcend their influence.

For Barbara, that process didn't happen overnight. It took consistent effort. At the end of her first session, I told her it was imperative that she 'follow her heart'. She had a hard time grasping that concept and took it as a throwaway line. The statement caused confusion, which triggered an appearance of Brash Barbara, who voiced her annoyance. She had no idea what she ultimately wanted to do with her life and felt powerless. To ease her mind, I told Barbara that getting in touch with her heart was the first step to following its lead. That meant connecting with her deepest feelings and paying attention to the things that brought her closer to joy. It was time for her to value her individual interests and genuine loves, rather than follow the lead of others. In short – she needed to keep her best interests at heart.

Barbara had buried many of her aspirations beneath several layers of guilt and shame. To compensate for her lack of worth, she created a glossy façade. Her identity was neither satisfying nor substantial, which merely caused frustration and sadness. Rather than express herself authentically with others, she attempted to put on a show. Although she was impressive, her actions slowly stripped away her self-respect. Barbara was reluctant to talk about her desires for fear of being mocked. If Barbara wasn't willing to believe in herself, her dreams would never come to life.

Reflecting on her past, Barbara pinpointed her most significant defining moments and determined the impact they had on her experiences. She began to see precisely where she sold out and gave her power away. Barbara realized how much credence she had given to the opinions and preferences of others instead of trusting her own feelings first.

Barbara longed to express herself fully in the world and dance through life, rather than hide in the shadows. Her inner strength sparked a vision of hope and she finally became humble enough to see her life could be totally different.

Eventually Barbara got in touch with her personal desires and genuine loves. But first she had to give herself permission to live the life of her dreams. She chose to claim her right to be happy, living her life for herself and not just to appease others. To truly honor her Soul and Spirit, Barbara needed to disengage from the general consensus and own her inner genius. Once that became her pledge, sensing her deepest feelings aligned her energy with True North.

With a natural talent for painting and drawing, and passion for landscape design, she changed careers at the age of thirty-nine, landing firmly on her feet. Giving up her job in sales and marketing, Barbara finally decided to use her gifts and acknowledge her preferences. Her love of gardening always exhilarated her Spirit and turning a blank sketchpad into a series of vibrant pictures brought her in touch with the essence of her Soul. When she entered that enchanted space, time stood still and she was completely present in the moment.

Barbara claimed her freedom by giving herself permission to do what she really loved to do and be who she authentically wanted to be. She was one woman who was brave enough to step out of the shadows into the light.

'When you are willing to set aside your personal inhibitions, you can break free from "the small story" of your life, relating to your upbringing and family, and live the bigger picture.'

Charting your course

Write your intention in your journal. Because you will be working specifically with your Authentic Self, use a declaration that aligns with being true to yourself.

Perhaps it is something like:

> **'During this level of the course I intend to be mindful of my genuine loves and personal preferences and notice how often I compromise my integrity.'**

Or you may prefer something more direct like:

> **'As I progress through this level of the course I intend to align with True North as often as possible.'**

Or

> **'I intend to be mindful of the fact that I am here to create a life that I love.'**

Choose statements that you are genuinely willing to abide by. Make your declaration of intent in the presence of your Higher Self and Soul, so you know you will make every effort to stand by your word.

Write this **Pocket Affirmation** *in your journal and post it in a prominent position to refer to as your daily mantra:*

**'I honor my Soul by celebrating my creativity
and nurturing my talents.
I am true to myself, knowing that I deserve
to live a life that I love.'**

Write the Key Words **Authenticity versus Self-Consciousness** *in your journal and contemplate them on a daily basis. Become conscious of which of the two you align with more often, to help you assess where you give your power away.*

Do the meditation for this level for a minimum of 15 minutes at least three times before moving onto the next level. You may want to record any insights in your journal.

The process

As an adult, you are free to chart your own course in life and choose who you want to be. Yet do you genuinely know that you are free to live a life that satisfies your Soul and brings you a deep sense of purpose? Are you more committed to doing what you believe you 'have to do' or are 'supposed to do' or following the call of your heart? If your head and your heart are at odds, that tug-of-war can play havoc with your emotions and leave you feeling spent. At which point, you may feel too tired or uninspired to do much of anything.

During this level of the course you are presented with an opportunity to move beyond that paradigm and get in touch with your Authentic Self. Your aim will be to shine a spotlight on the things you love and unleash more of your creativity.

Part of that process is sensing your deepest feelings as a gauge to see if you are following your intuition and aligning with True North. Remember the rule: When you are moving in a positive direction in life your emotions will be buoyant. When you are heading toward True North, your life is always graceful. If you go against the natural flow and push for control, things become a struggle.

During this level of the course you will also be working with your Soul's whispers to help you find your way. The first step to successfully reading your inner compass is to allow the perceptive, intuitive side of your nature to sense your course. Getting in touch with your inner senses is the key to honoring your True Self.

To do this successfully you must first monitor the intensity of your will, then honor your feelings as they emerge and be willing to trust them. Take small steps in the beginning to build that trust and lessen the influence of your negative Ego. Developing your intuition takes practice. The more you exercise it, the stronger your intuition becomes.

Write your answers to the following exercises in your journal.

EXERCISE 19 – PART A:

Keeping Your Best Interests at Heart

It is far too easy for us to live our lives based on what we think we 'should' do rather than follow the call of our heart. This next exercise will bring you in touch with genuine desires and preferences and steer you toward True North. Your aim during this level of the course is to focus your attention on what brings you joy and nurtures your natural talents.

How would your life change if you approached each day knowing that your priority was to keep your best interests at heart and incorporate more fun in your day? If obligation and duty took a back seat and fun, adventure and exploration came to the forefront, what would you do? With this exercise even the smallest things count.

Make a list of the things that nourish your Soul and awaken your Spirit. Include:

The things you enjoy and love to do

The things that inspire you

The things you are passionate about – causes, studies and interests

The things that naturally call you to adventure that are fun for you

The things you are naturally good at

The things you do that people compliment you on and admire you for

The things you have always wanted to do but never have

The things you are afraid to do but would love to do

Running through your list, choose at least one thing each day, over the course of the next week, and do it! Make a note of how that makes you feel. If you feel guilty, remind yourself you deserve to have fun and enjoy your life.

KEY COORDINATE NO. 14

In your journal, respond to the following in the separate section: Map of the Soul

What are the things you are the most passionate about?

What are you naturally good at?

What do you do that people compliment you on and admire you for?

EXERCISE 20 – PART A:

Acknowledging the Power of Trust.

Trust is one of the most powerful energies of creation that is available to you. The aim of this exercise is to help you recognize how important trusting yourself really is.

Take a moment to think about how much your life would change if you trusted yourself completely.

Ask yourself the following questions and make a few notes on how your life would change:

* How much time would you spend worrying, doubting or being confused?
* How much energy would you channel into being anxious?
* How often would you experience anxiety?
* How often would you manipulate and control rather than consciously and gracefully create.

Reflect on those questions and sense how powerful the energy of trust really is – it opens you up to receiving.

EXERCISE 20 – PART B:

Practicing Self-trust.

This following exercise will help you to run through the steps of building your trust. Look at making a simple decision at first to strengthen your confidence – but remember the risk needs to outweigh the benefits for trust to be an issue. Run through the steps given and then take action to follow through.

To gauge where your energy is constricted or expanded, sit with pen and paper and make notes under the following headings:

Mind: *Mentally run through the list of pros and cons of a particular choice. Make a list of the advantages and disadvantages to speculate and make a deduction.*

Body: *As you project what your life will be like should you choose a particular option, become aware of your body's muscular and nerve responses to see if you are tense or relaxed by this prospect.*

Feelings: *Get in touch with your feelings and watch which emotions come to the surface. Sense your gut level responses and hunches.*

Intuition: *Call on your intuition and sense your instinctive responses.*

The Combined Data: *Now you have gathered the information, run through your list of advantages and imagine what your life will be like if you choose a particular option. Be conscious if your energy expands or contracts on each level.*

EXERCISE 21:

Listening to the Whispers

During this level of the course recording your Soul-Speak will take a new twist. Ask your Higher Self and Soul to give you as many clues as possible in regard to the following questions. Your aim is to develop the perceptive side of your nature, which will allow you to hear your Soul's call to adventure.

Your Soul's whispers can be very subtle. They can easily be drowned out by the voice of logic or reason and intensity of your will. Stay receptive to life speak, dream speak and your intuitive senses.

Record the answers you receive through Soul-Speak to the following questions:

1. What do you need to focus your attention on to align with True North?
2. What do you need to let go of in the process?
3. Which talents and strengths do you need to focus on to bring you joy?

MEDITATION

The intention behind this meditation is to help you get in touch with your Authentic Self. Pay particular attention to the way you feel so you are familiar with the emotional resonance.

Find a comfortable position and begin to relax. Gently close your eyes.

Focus on your breathing and empty your mind of all thoughts. Take three deep breaths and exhale slowly.

Start by telling yourself that you can be anyone that you choose to be and then allow the images to come to you. Allow your imagination to expand and see yourself doing the things you love to do – being active in areas where you have strong interests. See yourself making a positive contribution through your work and creativity.

Let the images move you into the future. See yourself living a full and happy life, expressing your natural talents and abilities.

Take a few moments to sense how they feel.

As you attune to the energy of your Authentic Self, experience the love, joy, individuality and freedom that is available to you.

Once you can distinctly feel that resonance – take a deep breath and gently bring yourself out of the meditation.

Your checklist

1. Did you write in your journal on a regular basis to observe your thoughts and feelings?
2. Did you record the Soul-Speak outlined in Exercise 21?
3. Have you logged your insights, goals and aspirations?
4. Were you mindful of your intention throughout the course of your day?
5. Did you take time to contemplate the Divine Truth and the two Key Words?
6. Have you been using your Pocket Affirmation on a regular basis?
7. Have you taken time to meditate for a minimum of 15 minutes on at least three occasions?
8. Have you done your exercises and logged them?
9. Have you aligned with your Authentic Self to support your Heart's Desire?
10. If you haven't done any or all of these things then ask yourself – what stopped you?

You may be going into denial or avoidance around the topic for this particular level of self-discovery – what has your Ego been telling you? Those conversations reflect your limited beliefs about yourself. CHALLENGE THEM! Remember – your heart's desires are at stake.

LEVEL

9

During this level of the course you will learn more about the masculine and feminine sides of your nature, which either complement or conflict with one another. To recognize your full potential it is important to embrace and utilize the distinct qualities of both and bring them into balance.

If you depend on the assertive or masculine side of your nature to get what you want in life, you will compromise your depth of feeling and override your intuitive senses. When the feminine is favored, you will function in potential rather than building a strong foundation for personal success.

The Dance of Soul and Spirit – Masculine & Feminine Energies

DIVINE TRUTH: Life is a gift from God/Goddess/ All That Is and you are here to learn to receive.

KEY WORDS: Harmony versus Discord

Harmony is an integral part of recognizing that you are whole and complete. Being in a state of harmony aligns with equality and balance, whereas discord fuels Ego, fostering separation and control.

'To lead a balanced, abundant life, it is important to respect both the masculine and feminine sides of your nature. Both your assertive and receptive qualities must be synchronized to compliment one another and work in unison. Your Soul and Spirit then align in harmonious accord – this is the State of Dominion.'

Establishing harmony between the receptive and assertive sides of you creates an energetic flow that allows you to be fully self-expressed in the world while you feel inspired and loved. It will enable you to recognize that you are whole and complete, honoring both your Soul and Spirit.

The feminine energy relates to your Soul or essence – specifically to your feelings. It aligns with being and allowing. It encompasses imagination, intuition and inspiration – it is perceptive and receptive. The feminine nurtures – and allows itself to be nurtured, giving and receiving equally. The feminine is your power centre – 'your ability to' do something rather than the action you take. It perceives and conceives and is your creativity – the original energy. The feminine is the balance – the balancing of all things.

When you create using feminine energy, you gather content to force form and create a context to operate in. You put ideas together; you brainstorm and temporarily forget logic and reason. You start a thread in your imagination, let the inspiration carry you and see where it leads. Out of your imagination your feelings emerge. Your adrenaline starts flowing and your body responds. You create desire, which is the core of your creative energy. It works as a magnet that attracts whatever you imagine. Dipping into your creativity, you create and allow yourself to be created – you allow and are open to receive.

Your masculine energy dynamically creates and puts things into action – using logic and reason. It is the assertive, thinking side of your nature. As Spirit, it seeks and searches for meaning and understanding. The masculine instinctively provides and protects. It is the productive side of your nature that aligns with form rather than essence. It shapes and re-shapes, focuses and refocuses to form structure. The masculine way of creating is to build form in order to force content, which brings substance to the context of your reality.

To understand the different ways the two principles work, let's use the example of starting a new business. Creating through the feminine, you would imagine what the business would look like, visualize the type of environment you would like to work in and get a sense of how it feels to operate the company. You would then brainstorm ideas with friends or colleagues, get inspired about creative concepts and discuss future possibilities. Allowing your creative juices to flow, you might envisage the company logo, imagine your new website and flick through magazines to be inspired by the latest trends.

You could then research the market place and get a sense of what sort of clients you would like to attract. During the process, your imagination would continue to expand, while your desire builds. That inspiration would lift your emotional resonance and intensify your powers of attraction. Using this method, the energy generated would draw opportunities – you would gather content to force form. A friend may tell you about the ideal office space that has just come available or you might receive an unexpected call from someone who wants to engage your services. You gracefully attract the components that allow the business to manifest.

If you choose to create through the masculine, your aim would be to build form to gather content. Finding a space to rent and signing a lease might be a priority; along with printing business cards, putting an ad in the paper, launching a website, calling potential clients and hiring staff. Once that structure was in place, you would have a context or framework from which to operate. You would then attract clients to gather more content.

To experience a deeper and rewarding experience, incorporating both the masculine and feminine energies will align you with graceful creation. The assertive and receptive aspects of your make-up must be synchronized so that they operate together in an unobstructed way. If your masculine or feminine energy are diminished, you will struggle during the creative process.

To lead a balanced life, you need to value both sides of your nature and have an equal respect for essence and form – Soul and Spirit. Your Soul motivates your Spirit, which is active, always stretching to seek more light. Your Soul waits to be found, while your Spirit searches for deeper meaning and understanding of who you are and the world you live in.

The way you reconnect with your Soul is through your inner senses. Suspending your thoughts is an essential part of that process. How often do you stop thinking and simply perceive? Your feelings are beautiful tools for your expansion that sustain your relationship with All That Is. The true meaning of spirituality is having a living breathing relationship with God/Goddess/All That Is – The Essence or Source of all of creation. The key to fostering your spirituality is to harmonize your ability to give and receive equally, bringing things into balance.

When Soul and Spirit work in unison you naturally align with your Authentic Self and the path of graceful creation. That harmonious state allows your dreams and aspirations to take on form, synchronizing your desire, imagination and expectation. You sustain a vision that enables you to actively draw from the power and beauty of your essence, discovering more of your True Self.

When your Soul and Spirit work in harmony, your feminine energy guides you through your imagination, which awakens your feelings and generates your desire – the core of your creative energy. Your will motivates your desire into action. Behind any healthy imagination there is always a powerful will. You cannot separate the two. You must think in order to feel.

The key components are as follows:

FEMININE – BEING	MASCULINE – DOING
Essence	Form
Inspiration	Implementation
Imagination	Will
Intuition	Logic and Reason
Desire	Meaning and Understanding
Ability (the power that fuels)	Action
Receptive	Assertive
Creative	Productive
Feeling	Thinking
Nurturing and Being Nurtured	Protecting and Providing
Conceiving	Building
Perceiving	Evaluating
Allowing	Expressing

To balance the two sides of your nature, you need to recognize when you under or over emphasize the masculine or feminine. Your equilibrium can change in different areas of your life based on your self-image. For example, you may be very assertive, productive and fully self-expressed in your career; by contrast, your romantic relationships may be difficult.. You may also fluctuate at times, shifting your energy from one extreme to the next. The key is to harmonize your energy, allowing the feminine to conceive, sustain and balance your course. The masculine side of your nature then gracefully responds and is nourished and inspired throughout the process. By creating that sense of harmony you tap into the substance of your Soul and draw on your abilities to fuel and lift your Spirit. Bringing the two energies into alignment will enable you to create a life that reflects, goodness, truth and beauty – a life that you love.

No matter which sex you are, both the masculine and feminine principles support your creative process. Any discord that exists within you will reflect an imbalance in your physical world. This was the case with my client Kelly who needed to embrace and utilize more of her feminine energy to recognize her full potential and feel satisfied.

I talked in depth with Kelly about her childhood preference of wanting to be a boy. Although there were many things about being a girl she enjoyed, she felt boys had more power and freedom. Being brought up as a patriarchal daughter, she fell prey to the belief that men had the upper hand and therefore were somehow superior. It was time for Kelly to reassess her beliefs around the feminine energy and break away from the chauvinistic paradigm entrenched within the collective unconscious or the general consensus.

For Kelly to feel fulfilled she needed to retrieve her creativity, sensitivity and imaginative qualities and awaken the muse asleep in her Shadow. Kelly had judged these parts of her as being useless, favoring the use of logic and reason. As a consequence, she lacked inspiration and craved a more Soulful existence.

Kelly's early childhood dreams held the key to how beautiful life could be when she connected with her essence, celebrating her love and creativity. In recapturing her innocence, she became receptive to the idea that her life could be different if she retrieved the lost parts of herself. As fearful as she was, Kelly started to trust she had everything it took to be an assertive, strategic woman, who was also sensitive. She turned her attention toward being perceptive, imaginative and nurturing, breathing life into those parts of her.

Giving more credence to the feminine side of her nature, Kelly was willing to trust her intuitive senses and altered her choices. Slowly but surely Kelly grounded her capacity to balance all things. She gracefully aligned with a far more rewarding future where she felt supported and loved.

Kelly's transformation happened incrementally. It took thoughtful attention and consistent effort. It was like lifting a series of veils to uncover more of her power and beauty. The ultimate reward for Kelly was that she got in touch with her passion, which inspired her to take action. Rather than always pushing herself to maintain control in her life, she became far more receptive and her energy softened.

Responding to her genuine desires allowed her to resurrect some of her childhood dreams. Writing was one of the things on her list that she loved to do but never took seriously. With a newfound sense of worth, she gave herself permission to take pleasure in what she did and began writing a novel. Her imagination became a playground for her to explore her creativity and enjoy the fruits of her labor. The more Kelly immersed herself in her manuscript, the more of her talent came to life. For the first time since her early teenage years she was fully engaged in life.

Although Kelly originally feared not being taken seriously, the joy that she experienced from her new pursuits outweighed her reluctance to trust her feminine instincts. Much to her surprise she became more powerful, even though she was far more gentle and receptive. Her energy levels increased and she attracted a new circle of inspiring friends. By giving and receiving equally, she felt a sense of being complete. Kelly successfully managed to break free from a paradigm that had kept her feeling imprisoned, creating a life that equally honored her Soul and Spirit.

Charting your course

Write your intention in your journal. Because you will be working specifically with balancing the masculine and feminine energy, use a declaration that aligns with establishing harmony.

Perhaps it is something like:

'During this level of the course I intend to honor both sides of my nature.'

Or you may prefer something more direct like:

'I intend to focus primarily on being more receptive rather than forcing my will.'

Or

'As I progress through this level of the course I intend to be mindful of taking action and being more assertive.'

Choose statements that you are genuinely willing to abide by. Make your declaration of intent in the presence of your Higher Self and Soul, so you know you will make every effort to stand by your word.

Write this **Pocket Affirmation** *in your journal and post it in a prominent position to refer to as your daily mantra.*

> **'I am equally receptive and assertive, choosing a path of balance. I trust I am guided by my Soul and choose to honor my Spirit.'**

Write the Key Words **Harmony versus Discord** *in your journal and contemplate them on a daily basis. Become conscious of which of the two you align with more often, to help you assess where you give your power away.*

Do the meditation for this level for a minimum of 15 minutes at least three times before moving onto the next level. You may want to record any insights in your journal.

The process

During this level of the course your main focus will be on balancing the receptive and assertive sides of your nature. The first step is to tap into those energies by understanding them and identifying which side is dominant and which side may be diminished. The next step is to let the energies harmonize by making use of them.

Part of the process is following the gentle voice of your heart, which aligns with your Soul and essence and lifts your Spirit. This will help you sense your best course of action based on knowing your worth.

Following your Soul's Call to Adventure means being courageous enough to move forward and express yourself, even though you don't have all of the answers. Responding to that call relies on trust and confidence. Give yourself permission to make mistakes and learn from them, so you can build your trust and feel secure as you continue to grow. Connect with your Soul by feeling gentle, or lifting into joy. You will then draw the inspiration you need to spark your desire.

To fuel your Spirit, let yourself be strong, powerful and free to step into your radiance. Search and stretch for deeper meaning and understanding while you explore your creativity and expand your imagination. During that process, it is important to embrace the full range of your emotions. Connect more deeply with your Soul by sensing your goodness, truth and innate beauty. From that place choose to take action, crafting a life that you love.

Write your answers to the following exercises in your journal.

EXERCISE 22 – PART A:

Assessing Your Strengths

The aim of this exercise is to ascertain which aspects of the masculine and feminine energy are diminished in your character and which, in general, are stronger. It will help you distinguish which qualities you value and are in touch with and which you need to pay more attention to.

Run through the list below to gauge your level of strength using a scale of 1 (lowest) to 10 (highest).

FEMININE – BEING	Score 1–10	MASCULINE – DOING	Score 1–10
Essence		Form	
Inspiration		Implementation	
Imagination		Will	
Intuition		Logic and Reason	
Desire		Meaning and Understanding	
Ability (the power that fuels)		Action	
Receptive		Assertive	
Creative		Productive	
Feeling		Thinking	
Nurturing and Being Nurtured		Protecting and Providing	
Conceiving		Building	
Perceiving		Evaluating	
Allowing		Expressing	
TOTAL		TOTAL	

EXERCISE 22 – PART B:

Pinpointing Your Weaknesses

Each of the above masculine and feminine qualities are innate parts of your nature. In the same way physical muscles atrophy, if you don't use these qualities they will weaken. By answering the following questions, you can pinpoint which specific qualities you need to develop. Once you have your short list, consciously focus on each of them every day until you integrate them. Call on those parts of your nature in small ways as often as possible and practice using them.

Remember, setting a clear intention and consistently paying attention to it will bring it to life. Keep exercising those character traits to build and strengthen them. If you find it difficult, look at any negative beliefs you associate with those qualities and change them.

Did your highest total correspond with the feminine or masculine characteristics?

In that particular column, which specific three qualities reflect your lowest score?

In the opposite column, which specific quality reflects your lowest score?

EXERCISE 23 PART A:

Determining Signs Of Imbalance

To get an indication of where your masculine or feminine energy are either too strong or diminished, look for any of the following symptoms. Keep in mind that your energy may shift in different areas, so consider each arena of your life separately including:

Your career or vocation

Your romantic partnerships

Your relationships with men

Your relationships with women

How you approach your life generally

Answer yes or no to the following questions

- Do you avoid discussing your feelings and prefer to fix things or take action?
- Are you driven by other people's expectations and demands, functioning to get more and have more?
- Do you give more credence to men's opinions than women's opinions or take men more seriously?
- Are you chauvinistic?
- Do you see women as sex objects and men as power objects?
- Do you admire or value performance and appearance more than essence? Are you attached to looking good?
- Do you uphold your image at all costs, unwilling to admit when you feel weak or fall short of someone's requirements?
- Do you believe you have to be 'a particular way' as a woman or a man?
- Do you dominate the space, having to get everything right before you take a step?
- Do you have a strong need to take charge or assert your will?
- Are you rigid, needing to be in control?
- Are you judgmental, compartmentalizing people and things in your world?
- Do you suppress your feelings or disregard them and resist being vulnerable?
- Do you over analyze your feelings or situations?
- Do you see things in terms of black or white – either/or?
- Do you find it difficult to receive or be nourished and nurtured?

If you answered yes to a majority of those questions you probably have **Excessive masculine or a lack of feminine energy.**

Answer yes or no to the following questions:

- Are you alienated, with no true sense of where you are going, what you are doing or why you are doing it?
- Do you live from one moment, one day or one week to the next, without clear direction?
- Are you a victim or at the mercy of the life that you have created?
- Are you afraid or intimidated by the world or feel estranged from it?
- Do you view men or women, who are strong in their masculine energy, as aggressive, pushy, controlling, intimidating, foolish or insensitive?
- Are you quick to criticize, harbor negative emotion or blame?
- Do you gather content and lack form or structure? E.g. Have all of the qualifications or degrees and don't use them? Have all the information for a book and don't write it? Do all the research and gather all of the material for a project and don't do anything with it?
- Do you have a list of dreams and imaginings that never go anywhere or amount to anything or stagnate? Do you tell yourself you will do it someday or don't follow through?
- Do you function in potential, always coming up with ideas or schemes that never materialize?
- Is your personal identity diminished?
- Do you have a tendency to manipulate others out of weakness to get control?
- Does that manipulation become destructive? Do you hurt simply for the sake of hurting out of jealousy or to punish or get revenge?
- Do you overindulge and are weak willed?

If you answered yes to a majority of those questions you probably have **excessive feminine or a lack of masculine energy.**

Harmonizing Your Energy

Reviewing your answers from the following exercise, determine where you need to instigate balance. During this level of the course, become extremely conscious of when you are off kilter and shift your attention. Your aim is to alter your behavior so you establish harmony.

If you have too much masculine or a lack of feminine energy:

- Be conscious of being receptive as often as possible.
- Make a point of getting in touch with your inner senses to develop your perceptive abilities.
- Call on your intuition to sense your best cause of action, rather than solely relying on logic and reason.
- Stretch your imagination and do something creative just for the fun of it.
- Honor your feelings and move into gentleness as much as possible to presence more of your Soul and essence.

If you have too much feminine or a lack of masculine energy:

- Write an action plan and follow through.
- Whenever you feel as though the scales are tipped, bring up your assertive energy to reinstate your balance.
- Be conscious of using your will and consciously directing the course of your life as often as possible.
- Make clear choices and clearly state your intentions and take action.
- Do one or two things you have been putting off and follow through.
- Expand your thoughts and stretch for deeper meaning and understanding as often as possible.

MEDITATION

The intention behind this meditation is to help you create a representation of the masculine and feminine side of your nature. Your aim is use those images to receive information on where you need to lift your energy.

Find a comfortable position and begin to relax. Gently close your eyes.

Focus on your breathing and empty your mind of all thoughts. Take three deep breaths and exhale slowly. If your mind becomes active with idle thoughts, gently guide your attention back to the center of your being.

Allow yourself to go into a deeper state of relaxation. Allow your imagination to expand and imagine you are in your internal sanctuary. It may be a place of beauty in nature, or a temple built on a mountain. Imagine whatever feels right for you.

Engage with all of your senses, bringing the sights, smells, sounds and feelings to come to life.

Become aware of someone approaching you. As their image comes into view, you see a representation of the feminine side of you – your anima. She may appear as one of the archetypes or in a particular form that symbolizes her strengths.

Take a moment to study her features. Look at her face, hands, and body and become aware of her energy. Sense her power and beauty.

Ask her what feminine qualities you need to focus on to bring you into balance. Now take her hand and become aware of those qualities within her.

Close your inner eyes and sense those qualities awakening within you. Silently declare that you are willing to embrace them and feel her energy merging with yours.

When you are finished, open your inner eyes and notice a second figure approaching you.

As their image comes into view, you see a representation of the masculine side of you – your animus. He may also appear as one of the archetypes or a form that symbolizes his attributes.

Take a moment to study his features. Notice his face, hands and body and become aware of his energy. Sense his clarity and strong spirit.

Ask him what qualities you need to focus on to bring the masculine side of you into balance. Now take his hand and become aware of those qualities within him.

Close your inner eyes and sense those qualities awakening within you.

Silently declare that you are willing to embrace them and feel his energy merging with yours.

Feel them working together within you and sense the harmony of the two. Sense your imagination and your will coming into balance.

Take a few moments to focus on how that feels. Then take a deep breath and gently bring yourself out of the meditation.

Note: whenever you feel out of balance call upon the masculine or feminine parts of you and let their influence in. Meet with them regularly and get to know them.

Your checklist

1. Did you write in your journal on a regular basis to observe your thoughts and feelings?
2. Did you record any Soul-Speak?
3. Have you logged your insights, goals and aspirations?
4. Were you mindful of your intention?
5. Did you take time to contemplate the Divine Truth and the two Key Words?
6. Have you been using your Pocket Affirmation on a regular basis?
7. Have you taken time to meditate for a minimum of 15 minutes on at least three occasions?
8. Have you done your exercises and logged them?
9. Have you harmonized your masculine and feminine energy to support your Heart's Desire?
10. If you haven't done any or all of these things then ask yourself – what stopped you?

You may be going into denial or avoidance around the topic for this particular level of self-discovery – what has your Ego been telling you? Those conversations reflect your limited beliefs about yourself. CHALLENGE THEM! Remember – your heart's desires are at stake

LEVEL
10

During this level of the course you will turn your attention toward crafting a dream as a gateway for your self-expression. This will allow you to celebrate more of your creativity and enjoy the bounty of life. By nurturing and developing your aspirations you can build a platform to shine in the world that inspires your Soul and Spirit. There is power in your ability to foster what is right for you and hold a strong vision of a glorious future. If you are willing to take a stand for your dreams by following the call of your heart, you will attract everything you need to forge that creation.

Dream Weaving and Visioning – The Light Matrix

DIVINE TRUTH: The physical world is an illusion – so you can have as much of the illusion as you like.

KEY WORDS: Possibility versus Resignation

You live in a world that offers you unlimited opportunities. Believing in the power of the possible supports your dreams, hopes and aspirations, whilst resignation dulls the inner senses and closes the door to inspiration and growth.

> **'Your authentic dreams serve as a platform for you to express your strengths and talents, allowing you to grow in love and joy. Your dreams are your own special creation and you have the option to share those as a gift to the world.'**

No matter what your past reflects, you deserve to live a full and abundant life and the key to living that life is dreaming and visioning. According to universal law, you can be anyone, have anything and do anything you choose, with harm to none. It is your divine right to dream a dream and live that dream, by bringing it into creation. Dreaming is a vital part of your spiritual growth, which enhances your creativity.

Although there are times you have been inspired by your dreams, chances are you have also been disappointed when things didn't work out the way you wanted them to. You may have even felt as though you failed or were not good enough to keep up the momentum. Dreaming again might be more of a challenge for you, so it is important to remember that you do have the inbuilt capacity to make your dreams come true. Your success is not found in learning something new. It comes from utilizing what is already a part of you – your creativity.

Genuine dreams reflect your character, esteem, strengths and vitality. They allow you to craft a personal reality rich with joy, passion and individuality. They are the means for you to express your uniqueness and build a substantial identity. Keep in mind that your character is not something that you put on like a coat in the morning and take off at night. It is something that you live and breathe that is inherently a part of you. Getting clear on what lies beneath your aspirations is vital to creating a dream that will satisfy your heart.

You may have spent much of your energy in the past building dreams founded on other people's standards and were motivated by what you thought would impress or please them. If the contribution you make to the world is based solely on being admired, you are simply aiming to prove your worth.

Aspirations based on seeking outside validation, or getting attention, are not authentic dreams – they are aspirations that are formed to conceal your insecurities and will never fully manifest. The same applies if you attempt to live an idealized image to cover up your blockages or negative contracts and scripts. Dreaming is a means for you to have fun and consciously create success. If your dreams are too lofty, they have no relationship to your daily life and will remain a fantasy. Although you may have wonderful ideas, and it is healthy to stretch your thoughts, it is wise to consider your personal threshold – rather than jumping out of a plane and freefalling, use a parachute!

Building a substantial dream is very different from following a whimsy or creating a wish list. Fanciful thoughts of having lots of power, piles of money or fame and international status in order to make an impression have little to do with building character or substance. For that reason it is important to cherish and honor your authentic dreams by tending to them, rather than giving others the authority to endorse them.

The identity that you build in the world is a precious commodity. It is based on who you are, what you say, what you think and what you do. Holding a vision of the person you aspire to be will allow you to embrace the qualities you need to build a strong character. Your identity reflects your unique signature as an individual; it depicts your specific talents and distinct creativity. You are who you choose to be and your choices and decisions align with who you honestly believe and feel that you are. If you continually compromise your integrity by mimicking others or settling for mediocrity you will sabotage your dreams and dissuade your success.

After completing the exercises in Level 9, you are now more familiar with your Authentic Self. Having come this far on your Soul's journey, you have also uncovered more of your true potential. Your identity now encompasses more of who you really are from a spiritual perspective and you recognize that you are not just the personality you present to the world. By shining a torch on your True Self, your identity currently reveals the deeper, 'more real' you. You are more in touch with your Soul; therefore your imagination is your greatest guide to recreating your identity. It is a window into the realm of possibility, a place where dreams are inspired and born.

Everything that currently exists in your world is a reflection and expression of something more real. Beyond the time/space continuum and the physical world, there are subtle intangible planes that exist in higher dimensions. These subtler realms of existence are more real than the illusion of the physical world, including your dreams and imagination.

The realm of possibility, or the causal plane, is where all possibility waits in potential. It is the realm where everything originates – where all possible causes and effects exist simultaneously. Therefore every experience imaginable is potentially there for you to enjoy.

A possibility becomes a probability when you personally consider an experience to be viable in your world. If you believe that something is possible, but you don't believe it is likely to happen to you, it will not manifest. It is your fundamental beliefs that will energetically draw an experience into the tangible world of actuality.

The key to attracting anything is being receptive and genuinely willing to step into the reality. Your desire, imagination and core expectations need to be congruent in order to manifest your dreams, otherwise they will remain in the ether – outside time and space. The more attention you bring to a stream of thoughts, the more power you give them to manifest through the intensity of your feelings.

There is a vast amount of freedom for your Soul and Spirit to create beyond the physical world of logic and reason. When you enter the world of your subconscious during sleep, you explore what lies in the unconscious and the causal realm – or that which is not manifest. You link causes and effects and drop them into your physical reality. You also enter the astral realm where you investigate and test concepts to see how they relate, experimenting with different probabilities. They then bubble up from the unconscious and are made manifest during your waking state.

Through dreaming, you can liberate yourself from the past and open the door to optimal futures woven throughout the Light Matrix in your Soul's Hologram. It takes an open mind and an open heart to bring your desires and aspirations to life.

You begin by formulating your dreams with your thoughts and fueling them with your love and spirited passion. You then map your dreams with your subconscious, using your imagination and feelings to expand your beliefs and stretch your image. Those dreams and visions are then released into the world by activating your will and building your desire to receive their bounty. Staying receptive throughout that process will bring you in touch with more of your True Self, allowing your life to reflect greater value and deeper significance.

Remember, who you imagine yourself to be is who you will eventually become. If you imagine yourself as a person filled with fear and doubt you will be filled with fear and doubt. If you imagine yourself as someone who is filled with hope, inspiration and a sense of adventure, you become an inspiration.

Most dreams are dreams that fulfill your desires, needs and preferences. However there is another kind of dream, a luminous dream. A luminous dream can reveal more of who you really are. Luminous dreams are the ones you are committed to and stand by consistently, even if they don't manifest in the way you want them to. You strongly identify with them, continuing to commit to them no matter what. It is that level of commitment that makes a dream luminous.

They are dreams you can learn from that teach you more about yourself. Dreams that can guide you and offer you deeper understanding of your true potential, playing an integral part in your evolution. Those dreams are the ones that give you a reason to give up your old ways.

Aside from dreams you can also get valuable guidance and messages through visions. A vision is different from a dream in the way that it allows you to begin anew, disengaging from a past that no longer controls you. Vision is essential to creating a positive, successful future that liberates your Spirit. It aligns you with an optimal future, rich with new adventure. That future calls you to discover more of your True Self and enables you to glean more of your worth. Visioning can connect you with radiant futures illuminated by the passion of your Soul. It can hold the key to your success.

Vision and visioning exists outside of time and space and are detectable through Soul-Speak via your senses. Logic and reason can extinguish a vision, which may appear as a symbol or metaphor. Visioning is about sensing. It takes being receptive and allowing the vision to come to you through one of your familiar or unfamiliar senses. A vision may not necessarily come to you through sight but through sound or feelings. The key is to interact with your Soul, because it is your Soul's passion that will illuminate your vision and inspire your Spirit. In search of vision, you must be willing to let your Spirit soar; to reach and stretch in the pursuit of what is right and good and true.

Both luminous dreams and optimal futures are components of vision. There are seven features that distinguish an optimal future.

- An optimal future contains clear ongoing goals and challenges that enable you to stretch your strengths.
- An optimal future reflects a use of your talents and allows you to discover more of your potential and feel a sense of achievement.
- An optimal future enables you to stand strong, knowing you are autonomous while you integrate well with others, nurturing and sharing common goals.
- An optimal future allows you to take charge, but not control, with courage and conviction of heart.
- An optimal future provides you with a platform to experience love, joy and freedom as you discover more of your goodness, truth and beauty.
- An optimal future supports you in becoming the person you want to be, rather than manipulating others or relying on them to make you that way.
- An optimal future highlights your uniqueness and allows you to operate in harmony while you consider the greater good of all.
- An optimal future reveals your Authentic Self – you are no longer self-conscious, yet you are more conscious of your True Self and more consciously aware.

The Objector and the Protector

During your dreaming and visioning it is important that you remain mindful of how much you are willing to receive. At some point in your quest you will encounter and need to confront the Objector/Protector.

The Objector is associated with the dark side of your nature - it relates to Ego and the Shadow. It will often show up as the 'dream stealer' and the saboteur. The Objector is the part of you that continually reminds you what you can't have. It is the little voice in the back of your mind that sounds like a critical parent that is constantly objecting. You need to be very conscious of what your Objector says while you are in search of your vision and while you are visioning. Those 'yes buts' and 'what ifs' are voiced by the Objector who has all the reasons 'why not'. It will tell you why you can't have what you want and that you can't win.

The Objector resists change and objects to anything that is different than what you currently experience. It keeps addictions, old habits and old patterns in place. When you eliminate your sense of not deserving, or not being good enough, the Objector brings it back. It reminds you of your hurts and keeps you locked in the paradigm of having to have control. If you tear down your defense shield it will attempt to put it back and when you unravel your Dark Matrix it will come along to repair it – so if you are wondering why your life doesn't change, or why your dreams haven't come into fruition, look to see if the Objector is at work. The Objector/Protector protects you by holding your armor in place and keeping you in your 'comfort zone'.

There is a positive side to that part of you that emerges as the Protector /Objector and aligns with your Higher Self and the Objective Observer. It knows when you are operating out of Ego and when you are feeding your self-righteousness or arrogance. It will remind you when you are caught up in fantasy and will protect you from being destructive.

The Protector can protect you by stopping you. It knows where you give your power away and will tell you when you have rested too long or pushed too hard. The Protector knows the obstacles on your path and what you need to let go of so you can open up to receiving more. This aspect of your nature can teach and guide you in the same way a loving parent would. The Protector/Objector protects you by keeping you on track and showing you where you compromise your integrity and worth, encouraging you to receive. Keeping this distinction in mind will help you avoid sabotaging your dreams. When you encounter the Objector – shift your energy and realign your focus with the Protector.

If you are committed to your dreams and consistently nurture them, you will achieve your goals. Therefore be conscious of where your attention goes and what you devote your energy to. If you love yourself enough you will bypass the Objector and give yourself permission to direct your energy into something that satisfies your Soul and lifts your Spirit. The choice is always yours. So choose happiness and focus on the things in this world that bring you joy. Anything that is born with love reaps the greatest rewards.

Charting your course

Write your intention in your journal. Because you will be working specifically with dreaming and visioning, use a declaration that aligns with exploring the realm of possibility.

Perhaps it is something like:

> **'During this level of the course I intend to weave a beautiful dream.'**

Or you may prefer something more direct like:

> **'As I progress through this level of the course I intend to focus on vision and visioning and will take quiet time to be receptive.'**

Or

> **'I intend to dream a luminous dream that highlights my strengths, talents and uniqueness.'**

Choose statements that you are genuinely willing to abide by. Make your declaration of intent in the presence of your Higher Self and Soul, so you know you will make every effort to stand by your word.

Write this **Pocket Affirmation** *in your journal and post it in a prominent position to refer to as your daily mantra.*

> **'Love, joy and abundance now comes to me in endless ways. The people in my world are a link in the chain of my success.'**

Write the Key Words **Possibility versus Resignation** *in your journal and contemplate them on a daily basis. Become conscious of which of the two you align with more often, to help you assess where you give your power away.*

Do the meditation for a minimum of 15 minutes at least three times before moving onto the next level in order to ground the imagery. You may want to record any insights in your journal.

The process

During this level of the course your main focus will be on dreaming and visioning. Now that you have worked with your blockages and scripts, you are ready to weave a dream born of the heart. You may not have cleared away all of your negativity but you have made enough progress to build a dream that supports your Authentic Self. Not a whimsy or a fantasy but a genuine dream you can call your own and start living.

Selecting a path that challenges your skills is an essential component. Your Soul is calling you to grow, so you can uncover more of your True Self. Whenever you take on anything new in the world, you learn more about yourself. So stay open to fully exploring your untapped potential.

The way you formulate a dream is by getting in touch with your passion and aligning with True North – the path of graceful creation. Despite your age, it is never too late to acknowledge your talents and develop your creativity. Give yourself permission to be adventurous during the creative process and take pleasure in what you do. You will then naturally engage with the magical child and curious adolescent that are still a living, breathing part of you. That influx of joy will allow you to create a dream that is inspired by your heart. You came into this world with all the individual attributes it takes to be successful. Just be very careful not to let other people's opinions deter you from your course.

Imagination and passion are often dampened by conformity or doubt. There is power in your ability to take a stand for what you believe in. Genuine hope only ever exists if you sanctify your dreams. To transform your world, you need to hold high expectations of being fulfilled and allow your dream to unfold gracefully with patience.

With a dream in your heart, you can let your desire fuel your journey. If you take one small step at a time and practice being grateful, opportunities will continue to present themselves. Just don't be attached to how things showed up. Remain receptive to abundance and be willing to fully participate. Commitment and consistency are important keys to producing results; once the elements of your dream are clearly in your thoughts, set short and long-term goals to ground the process.

To keep you both motivated and inspired, use creative visualization on a daily basis. Remember it is your desire, imagination and expectation that will ultimately manifest the things that you want. It will help you stay focused on who you are becoming and not just who you've been in the past, which will align you with positive futures.

Write your answers to the following exercises in your journal.

EXERCISE 24 – PART A:

Formulating your Dreams

The following exercise will help you to pull together the threads of your dream and weave a beautiful tapestry of the life you desire. The aim of the exercise is for you to clarify what you would like to create and what you would like to experience. It is wise to focus more on the essence of your success rather than merely consider the trappings, otherwise your dreams will lack the depth and substance vital for nourishing your Soul and Spirit.

The question to ask yourself as a catalyst is:

'If I loved myself completely in this moment, how different would my life be? What would I finally let myself do and have and who would I choose to be?'

To give up your old ways and be open to change, be mindful of the presence of the Objector/Protector. Refrain from using your past as a reference for what is possible; be humble enough to know that things can be different.

EXERCISE 24 – PART B:

Enhancing your Dream

Drawing from what you have written, make a shortlist to hone your focus. This exercise will also bring you more in touch with your passion, which sparks activity.

Start by reflecting on what you will be doing when your life is fulfilled and you're living the life you've always wanted to live.

What makes you happy?

What do you love and stirs your enthusiasm?

What triggers passion within you?

What is your creative expression?

What will you be doing more of in the future that you love to do now?

After reviewing the list above, write out a few of your goals to ground the exercise.

What do you specifically want to accomplish long-term?

What do you want to achieve in the short-term that supports that dream?

KEY COORDINATE NO. 15

In your journal, respond to the following in the separate section: Map of the Soul

In a one-line statement, list 3 prime achievements that standout in your dreams.

EXERCISE 25:

Creating a Luminous Dream

The intention behind this exercise is to further explore the terrain of your dreams in search of a thread to an optimal future. Your aim is to muse over your goals and aspirations to create a luminous dream.

Sit quietly and reflect on the dreams you uncovered during the previous exercise.

Considering the following components, pinpoint the area of your life where they most apply. This will help you create the foundation for a luminous dream.

Which area of your dreams strongly reflects your dignity and character?

Which area of your dreams reflects your strengths and talents?

Where do you have the most vitality – what do you naturally bring life to?

What are your priorities – where do you primarily focus your attention?

Which part of your dreams are you consistently committed to - no matter what?

Which part of your dreams do you most strongly identify with?

What is your vision in that area?

Which of your strengths and talents would you like people to recognize you for?

With those strengths that you know you have, how would you ultimately like to express them?

KEY COORDINATE NO. 16

In your journal, respond to the following in the separate section: Map of the Soul

What is your luminous dream?

EXERCISE 26 – PART A:

Creating a Dream.

Everyday for the next week, take 10 – 15 minutes a day to write out a small piece of your dream. As you continue to write, expand the dream as much as you can. Whether it is a luminous dream or something smaller you want to create, build your vision in increments. It may be a loving relationship or career filled with abundance and joy, or it may be something like buying a house or travelling to exotic places to adventure and explore. It could be a luminous dream where you are working with people to help them heal, grow or be inspired. Whatever your dream, incorporate as much detail as you can and bring vitality to it.

At the end of the week write a clear intention or vision statement to crystallize your dream in the back of your thoughts.

EXERCISE 26 – PART B:

Building a Dream.

This exercise is an ongoing 'mini meditation' that will help to program your subconscious mind. Use the same dream you defined in the previous exercise.

Choose a favorite piece of music that puts you in a relaxed state of mind – preferably without lyrics. Every day for the next week take 10 – 15 minutes a day to close your eyes and imagine yourself living out your dream. Go through the motions of being in the dream, rather than watching the dream as an observer.

In the same way that a television series runs, live out your dream in episodes. Each day, pick up precisely where you left off the previous day. Continue to live it in small parts as the scenario in your life expands. You may want to jot down a few brief notes about where you left off, to sharpen your focus.

MEDITATION

The intention behind this meditation is to create a temple of Soul or dream temple – an inner sanctuary that becomes your place to vision. Here you can connect with optimal futures and luminous dreams. Once you lay the track, you can go there any time you need to receive insight or be inspired. It is a place for you to commune with your Soul and listen to its voice.

Your aim is stay receptive to what comes to you through your inner senses. Rather than see your vision, you may feel or sense an impression that sparks inspiration. You may even hear music, symbols or colors. Just be with what comes to you and let it unfold.

Find a comfortable position and begin to relax. Gently close your eyes.

Focus on your breathing and empty your mind of all thoughts. Take three deep breaths and exhale slowly. If your mind becomes active with idle thoughts, gently guide your attention back to the center of your being.

Allow yourself to go into a deeper state of relaxation.

Let your imagination expand and imagine you are making your way through the beauty of nature to your temple. It may be built on a mountain or in a clearing in the middle of a forest – imagine whatever feels right for you. Engage with all of your senses, bringing the sights, smells, sounds and feelings to life.

Call in the presence of your Soul and gently surrender to being in a state of innocence. Sense your mind expanding and your heart opening. Sit quietly and allow yourself to be impressed. Take a few quiet moments to focus on what comes to you and allow yourself to simply be.

Once you have received a glimmer or wave of inspiration – take a deep breath and gently bring yourself out of the meditation.

Your checklist

1. Did you write in your journal on a regular basis to observe your thoughts and feelings?
2. Did you record any Soul-Speak?
3. Have you logged your insights, goals and aspirations?
4. Were you mindful of your intention?
5. Did you take time to contemplate the Divine Truth and the two Key Words?
6. Have you been using your Pocket Affirmation on a regular basis?
7. Have you taken the time to meditate for a minimum of 15 minutes on at least three occasions?
8. Have you done your exercises and logged them?
9. Have you been dreaming and visioning to support your Heart's Desire?
10. If you haven't done any or all of these things then ask yourself – what stopped you?

You may be going into denial or avoidance around the topic for this particular level of self-discovery – what has your Ego been telling you? Those conversations reflect your limited beliefs about yourself. CHALLENGE THEM! Remember – your heart's desires are at stake.

LEVEL

11

During this level of the course you will focus your attention on creating an intimate relationship with your Optimum Future Self. Strengthening that connection will help you to manifest your luminous dreams and align with radiant futures.

Throughout this level you will be particularly mindful of who you are becoming in the world. You are at the center of your creation and the way you view your potential is crucial. Which probable future you attract depends on how much of your power and beauty you are prepared to embrace and how you genuinely feel about yourself. Your aim is to move beyond mediocrity and claim more of your magnificence.

Creating Magic and Miracles – Optimum Future Self

DIVINE TRUTH: You are a part of the process of evolution – you are who you are becoming and not just who you have been.

KEY WORDS: Magnificence versus Mediocrity

Stepping into your magnificence allows you to acknowledge the power and beauty of your Soul and Spirit. That sublime splendor is inherent within each and every one of us. Settling for mediocrity will only diminish your growth and curtail your freedom.

'If you stay focused on what inspires you, rather than what depletes your Spirit, you will move progressively forward. It is therefore important to develop a vision of your Optimum Future Self as a reference point to build your dreams on.'

Based on the premise that time and space don't exist beyond the physical world, everything in creation already exists as it continues to evolve and grow. As challenging as it is to fully grasp that concept, it amplifies the fact that all things are possible. Your Future Selves already exist in the realm of possibility as a living, breathing aspect of your consciousness.

Your potential futures consist of a multitude of possibilities that range from nightmare realities, living in mediocrity and optimal futures. Each future radiates a particular resonance, along a frequency of vibration, which releases waves in various waveforms that have impact on you now. Resonance is an attractor. Once within its field of force, you can attract things magically and miraculously.

The theory that most people accept is that the past leads to the present. Yet, the metaphysical/spiritual paradigm is based on the future creating the present over the backdrop of the past. Since the future creates the present, every future has impact now. The 'greater you' has influence on who you are in the moment. Consciously creating a positive, joyful future through dreaming will augment your current reality because your attention moves toward who you are becoming. By doing so, you use the power of resonance to shift your perception and attract new experiences.

You cannot think without feelings and you cannot feel without thinking – they are the raw materials that create your reality. The thoughts, images and feelings behind your experiences form streams of consciousness that hold a particular resonance or frequency. They are like energetic threads that are impressed with information woven through the Dark and Light Matrix in your Soul's Hologram. Each of those threads holds your personal resonance, which constitutes how you appear in your world and what you attract. Success has its own resonance, its own frequency, as do abundance prosperity and love.

Each of your 'probable selves' also has their own resonance or frequency, which aligns you with varying experiences. Once you generate the resonance of success, it changes you. If you can move into that resonance, or alter your frequency, it dissolves blockages from your past and you create yourself anew.

The way you harness that energy is by experiencing and exploring your feelings with depth and intensity – moving into the expansive range of emotions. You can then create a field of force that will lift you to a position where the gift of your Soul's legacy awaits you – the unique gifts that you were born with. Remember, your Light Matrix is made up of your fortune. It holds more of your unique talents, creativity, strengths and character, which align with your ultimate destiny. It is a state of awareness you reach where you experience a deep sense of meaning and purpose in your life. Lifting your resonance to that degree expands your image and opens you to the majesty and grace of your optimal futures.

Your Soul's Blueprint includes alternatives, which allow you to be fully self-expressed and experience a full and rewarding life. Your true destiny is to be all that you can be, assigning your unique signature to the dreams and visions you create. Whether your desire is to build a substantial business empire or create rewarding relationships; to attract the experience, it all comes down to just how open you are to experiencing the reality and how much you are willing to receive. On one level you've already created exactly what you want. There is a future you that exists in the realm of possibility living the life you've always dreamed of. Your Future Self has everything it takes to generate and maintain that reality. It is a matter of you realizing that those qualities exist within you now.

The step to manifesting your dreams is to embrace the qualities of already being there. If your thoughts and feelings align with your Optimum Future Self, and you sense those qualities in the moment, you will gradually integrate them into your character. That's how the principle of resonance works. The more you sense and own the qualities of your Optimum Future Self, and connect with their resonance or energy field, the more you will be drawn into the experience. To live it – you first have to feel it. So the key is to pay attention to the vibrancy of your emotions – are they expansive or constrictive on the scale of resonance?

Your experiences are determined by your beliefs and expectations. Those assumptions will either imprison you or liberate you from the Dark Matrix. To change your expectations, you need to form a clear mental image of the person you want to be and intensify your desire. Hold the sense that you are already that person. By harmonizing your energy with your Optimum Future Self you will attract the experience. The more sensitive and receptive you become to their energy the faster the changes in your world will occur.

The two key principles of 'intention' and 'attention' are fundamental when it comes to determining which Future Self you align with. Where you focus your attention, along with your underlying intention, will sway the dial of destiny. If the range of possibilities you hold in your mind is reduced your power also diminishes. The choice is always left up to you. Amongst your futures are your radiant futures, which are the terrain of luminous dreams and your Optimal Future Self.

It is not enough to visualize your Future Self; you need to establish an intimate relationship with it through your inner senses. To ground its resonance – feel what your Future Self feels. Stepping into the feeling of having your heart's desires fulfilled makes your future dreams a current reality. It is important to be open to miracles and be willing to accept them when they manifest. A miracle in this case is defined by receiving more that what you expect. You actually create those miracles and therefore it is essential that you claim responsibility for them when they occur.

If you are disciplined in the practice of holding a vision of your Optimum Future Self, you can consistently be inspired by the experience. It will open you up to giving and receiving more freely, bringing you in touch with the abundance that is readily available to you. The way you see yourself will either open you up, or close you down, to the wonderful opportunities that are always there in the waiting.

When you hold a positive self-image your feelings will respond, which is why it's important to continually practice self-acceptance. If you chastise yourself for not being enough in the moment, you will sabotage your progress by lowering your emotional resonance.

Building a vision of your Optimum Future Self has nothing to do with creating an idealized image of perfection. It is best to allow the image to intuitively come to you, rather than constructing a glossy vision of the 'perfect you.' Focus on the essence of the person you want to be and allow your Future Self's physical appearance to reflect those qualities. Remember, they are not just a figment of your imagination; they are a living breathing part of you that already exists in creation. Your aim is to key into their vibration, or emotional resonance, to boost your powers of attraction and experience more love, joy, individuality and freedom.

If you can imagine and deeply feel what an experience is like, then you can attract a series of events that will call it into being. Anything you can imagine is possible. All transformation begins with an intense desire to transform – you must be genuinely willing to change and be different.

Before you can begin to change, you have to let go of the past. Your Future Self is always ready to materialize, but unless you are free of doubt or reservation, and willing to step into their shoes, the reality will not manifest. Therefore, your attitude should be one that reflects commitment.

If you are devoted to becoming more of your True Self, you need to turn your back on any contrary conversations that don't support the fulfillment of your dreams. Don't rehash your old worn-out scripts or repetitive jargon. Any dialogue, whether it is in your mind or voiced in the world, that doesn't contribute to your vision needs to be rejected. To stay on track, be mindful of the tone of your conversations with your friends, colleagues and family. Whenever you focus on your past disappointments or complain about your present situation, you keep your grievances alive. It is important you accept, rather than resist, where you are in the moment and stay focused on your Optimum Future Self. Steer your attention away from what is missing and focus on what you want.

A living imagination will intensify your progress – it is the impetus of creation. The key is focused attention. It will help you develop a more active, dynamic relationship with your future. You already have a relationship with your Future Self – but which one? Is it beneficial or unfavorable? Are you still projecting your past into the future or creating new vistas of possibility?

It is vitally important you don't have an investment in keeping the past alive. Remember, the future creates the present; so which future do you perceive to be more real? If your relationship with your Optimum Future Self is healthy, you will breathe life into that reality. Establishing greater intimacy and rapport will create opportunities for you. It is through that relationship that you can ultimately create transcendence – it can lift you out of the Dark Matrix.

Through dream weaving and visioning you can create new maps to new futures, changing the matrix of your reality. Not just creating a better future, or a higher level of achievement, but aligning with a destiny that lets you consciously evolve and fulfill your Soul's purpose. During that quest, your affinity with your Future Self is crucial. Even though that path poses certain challenges, you need to be able to uncover both your weaknesses and strengths so you can utilize them. Success is not just about the trappings; it is about building character and being happy.

Although the future motivates change, you are not striving for perfection or seeking a future that 'fixes' your past or present. Your future is not a reward – it is a platform for your expression that you create. Your aim is to create a future with a resonance that supports love, joy, individuality and freedom that has impact on you now.

When you work with your Future Self in the moment, you can access the light of hope and love. Keep in mind that the power of the possible and probable are more real than the illusion of the physical world, along with the subconscious and unconscious.

Recognizing the power of the possible, you can fully embrace a future where you are loved and loving, experiencing the goodness, truth and beauty of your Soul and Spirit. You can explore the magic and wonder of your creativity that can serve as a remedy to overcome negativity and debilitating emotions. By connecting with optimal futures, you can allow yourself to simply be, as you discover more of your True Self. Taking that stand enables you to grow exponentially as you become more conscious of your magnificence.

Your luminous dreams will appear far more achievable if you embrace them in the moment with your thoughts, imagination and feelings – backed by clear choices. Even the small choices you make on a day-to-day basis are extremely important. They warrant which Future Self you align with. Your point of power is in the moment – because your choices act as the bridge between your past and a bright new future. Every choice and decision you make is based on how you see yourself and who you believe you are. That is why it is essential you hold a strong image of your Optimum Future Self and make choices that support your growth.

Having an intimate relationship with your Future Self involves paying attention to detail, which requires patience. Your opportunities automatically increase if you stop projecting your doubts into the future and stay humble and receptive to things being different. If you feel stuck or confused, you can always turn to your Optimum Future Self for wise counsel. You can call upon them as a guide and ally. After all, they have already navigated the course and know the best approach to take. Using your imagination is the way you connect with them. All you need to do is imagine your Optimum Future Self and then ask what they would do in your situation. The answer that comes is usually a liberating one, if you let it come to you through your intuitive senses.

Charting your course

Write your intention in your journal. Because you will be working specifically with your Optimum Future Self, use a declaration that aligns with claiming more of your magnificence.

Perhaps it is something like:

'During this level of the course I intend to attune to the resonance of my Optimum Future Self as often as possible.'

Or you may prefer something more direct like:

'As I progress through this level of the course I intend to draw on the strengths and talents of my Optimum Future Self.'

Or

'I intend to steer my attention toward optimal futures.'

Choose statements that you are genuinely willing to abide by. Make your declaration of intent in the presence of your Higher Self and Soul, so you know you will make every effort to stand by your word.

Write this **Pocket Affirmation** *in your journal and post it in a prominent position to refer to as your daily mantra.*

'I call upon the power and beauty of my Optimum Future Self. Through her/him, I align with an endless stream of abundance and grace.'

Write the Key Words **Magnificence versus Mediocrity** *in your journal and contemplate them on a daily basis. Become conscious of which of the two you align with more often, to help you assess where you give your power away.*

Do the meditation for this level for a minimum of 15 minutes at least three times before moving onto the next level to ground the resonance of your Optimum Future Self. You may want to record any insights in your journal.

The process

Using the principles of 'intention and attention' during this level of the course will help you to stay on track. If you constantly affirm that you are open to experiencing more, you will start to see results. During that process, you need to continually give up what no longer serves you and hold the vision of what you wish to experience. It is important that you *know* you are good enough to receive the bounty of your Future Self. Above all, believe in the magic of your luminous dreams; they are a bridge to your optimum futures.

If you align your thoughts with your idealized self, rather than your Optimum Future Self, your experience will be shallow. Your Ego's interpretation of the vision will emphasize the level of your performance and appearance rather than your depth of character and substance. Qualities such as courage, confidence, wisdom, clarity and commitment are all aspects of the person you are ultimately becoming. The more of your Future Self's light or attributes you claim, the more radiant your future becomes.

To master the art of graceful creation, you need to allow things to develop organically, in stages, while you stay focused on your desired outcome. You are growing with each step you take. As you strengthen the relationship you have with your Optimum Future Self, you will gravitate toward the pinnacle in your Soul's Hologram. This is the realm of optimal futures and personal greatness, which resonates with love, joy, individuality and freedom.

Stay mindful of the Objector/Protector. It will sabotage your progress if your commitment to change isn't strong enough. Consciously creating a rapport with your Optimum Future Self on a daily basis will sharpen your focus.

Establish an intimate relationship with your Future Self by using your inner senses – feeling their presence in the moment. Your aim is to key into their vibration, or emotional resonance, to boost your powers of attraction.

The more sensitive and receptive you become to your Future Self's energy, the faster changes will occur in your world. Keep in mind that if you repeatedly visualize yourself already living out your heart's desires, you will eventually bring those images to life. Be willing to explore the intensity and depth of your emotions to create the force field that aligns you with their resonance.

Write your answers to the following exercises in your journal.

EXERCISE 27:
Building A Vision Of Your Optimum Future Self

This exercise will help you connect with your Optimum Future Self. Keep in mind that you are not constructing an idealized image of perfection. Focus on the essence of the person you are becoming and allow their appearance to reflect those qualities.

Sit quietly; expand your imagination and still your thoughts. Take a few quiet moments to reflect on your luminous dreams and optimal futures.

Allow an image to come to you of your Future Self and sense their energy.

Are they confident, wise, happy, adventurous, creative, joyful, powerful or loving? What qualities do they emanate?

What are their preferences and primary focus? What is important to them in their life?

EXERCISE 28:

Forming an Alliance with your Optimum Future Self

The following exercise will help you to align with your Optimum Future Self and call on them for guidance. By acknowledging their qualities and utilizing those strengths in your current reality, you will begin the transformation process.

Remember – the main step to getting there is to embrace the qualities of already being there.

Look at the area of your life that you have chosen to transform. Sit quietly and visualize your Future Self.

What would they do differently in your situation?

What strengths would they draw upon?

What significant choices would they make?

EXERCISE 29:

Building a Bridge to your Future Self

The aim of this exercise is to set up a link between you and your Optimum Future Self.

For the next seven days, just before you go to sleep each night, ask your subconscious to connect you with your Optimum Future Self during the dream state.

Make a request that you work with your Future Self to clear the path to manifesting your luminous dream.

As you drift off to sleep, repeat three times, 'I will wake up, more and more in my luminous dream.'

The following day, look for signals that your dream is appearing and unexpected opportunities or signs through Soul-Speak.

MEDITATION

This meditation will help you to attune to the resonance of your Optimum Future Self. They may appear to be many years older or just a few months older. Your aim is stay receptive to the images that come to you and engage through your inner senses. Aligning with the resonance of your Optimum Future Self on a regular basis will impact your current reality because resonance is an attractor, once within its field of force, you can attract things magically and miraculously.

During this meditation, you will enter the temple of Soul or dream temple you created in Level 10. It is here that you can meet with your Future Self. This is your inner sanctuary, your place to connect with optimal futures and luminous dreams.

Find a comfortable position and begin to relax. Gently close your eyes. Focus on your breathing and empty your mind of all thoughts.

Take three deep breaths and exhale slowly. If your mind becomes active with idle thoughts, gently guide your attention back to the center of your being.

Allow yourself to go into a deeper state of relaxation. Let your imagination expand and imagine you are making your way through the beauty of nature to your temple. Engage with all of your senses, bringing the sights, smells, sounds and feelings to life.

Call in the presence of your Optimum Future Self and gently surrender to being in a state of innocence. Sense your mind expanding and your heart opening.

Take a few quiet moments to focus on the images and impressions that come to you through your inner senses. Open up to the energy of your Future Self. Sense the intensity of their power and beauty. Note any particular qualities that stand out and become aware of their strengths.

Make a connection through all of your senses and become aware of the specific frequency of vibration or resonance that your Future Self emanates. Connect with their field of energy by sensing their essence. Align with their resonance by exploring the depth of your emotions. Feel them intensely.

Take a few moments to seek counsel, guidance or inspiration. Sit with them or walk and talk with them. Once you have completed the exchange, take a deep breath and gently bring yourself out of the meditation.

Note: You can use this as a micro-meditation at any time during the day when you need to shift your energy. Simply hold a cameo image of your Optimum Future Self in the back of your mind and sense it's resonance. Take slow deep breaths and imagine you are connecting with their energy field. Feel it as intensely as you can and use this simple affirmation: 'I am who I am becoming and not who I have been.'

KEY COORDINATE NO. 17

In your journal, respond to the following in the separate section: Map of the Soul.

In a short, succinct sentence, describe the qualities of your Optimum Future Self.

Your checklist

1. Did you write in your journal on a regular basis to observe your thoughts and feelings?
2. Did you record any Soul-Speak?
3. Have you logged your insights, goals and aspirations?
4. Were you mindful of your intention?
5. Did you take time to contemplate the Divine Truth and the two Key Words?
6. Have you been using your Pocket Affirmation on a regular basis?
7. Have you taken time to meditate for a minimum of 15 minutes on at least three occasions?
8. Have you done your exercises and logged them?
9. Have you been focusing on your Optimum Future Self to support your Heart's Desire?
10. If you haven't done any or all of these things then ask yourself – what stopped you?

You may be going into denial or avoidance around the topic for this particular level of self-discovery – what has your Ego been telling you? Those conversations reflect your limited beliefs about yourself. CHALLENGE THEM! Remember – your heart's desires are at stake.

LEVEL

12

During this level of the course you will revise the principles you have learnt and pull together all of the pieces of the puzzle to reveal your Soul's Purpose and create the Map of your Soul. You can then use this map to navigate your way to the pinnacle point in your Soul's Hologram, aligning you with your Ultimate Destiny.

Your aim is to reflect on your Key Coordinates and piece them together to form a clear path to your Optimum Futures. Following that course will shift your resonance and lift you into the Light Matrix in your Soul's Hologram, allowing you to enter a state of love, joy, individuality and freedom.

Discovering your
True Purpose –
Your Soul's Destiny

DIVINE TRUTH: You can be anyone, have anything and do anything you choose, with harm to none.

KEY WORDS: Enlightenment versus Illusion

Enlightenment comes from knowing your True Self. It means ending the pretense that you are merely physical and remembering who you really are. From a higher perspective, the physical world is nothing more than an illusion. You are in the process of discovery that theory as your truth.

> **'You are an aspect of God/Goddess/All That Is, and as you grow, you are becoming more so. Each reflection or facet of your Soul exhibits contrasts – shades or degrees of light or energy. You are simply growing and expanding to discover more of your True Self.'**

By this stage of your journey you will have already created a stronger connection with your Authentic Self and are now able to distinguish when you are following True North – the path of graceful creation. That course leads to a state of Dominion or living in complete harmony with God/Goddess/All That Is. That is your ultimate destiny – to return to the Source. You are not separate; nor have you ever been. You are simply asleep to the full majesty of your Soul and in the process of going home.

Your attention is like a laser that brings life to what exists within that point of focus. Everything imaginable is there in the offering and the reality you want is no more than a belief away. Your future is calling to you; it beckons you to claim more of your goodness, truth and beauty to reveal more of your Soul's splendor.

You are free to be anyone, have anything and do anything you choose, with harm to none. When you fully embrace that Divine Truth as your own, you dismantle the Dark Matrix you originally created by realizing your full potential and knowing your inherent worth.

The components of your Dark Matrix pinpoint precisely what stands in the way of you being fully empowered. Keep in mind they are obstacles you have constructed. They are hurdles you placed on your path to help you develop your strengths and talents. They are there as challenges for you to overcome and not insurmountable problems.

You have come into this life to clear the blockages from your energy field by mastering your life's lessons. Consciously working with those lessons will show you where you are on or off course and will point to your Soul's purpose or life's focus. By choosing that exalted path you honor both your Soul and your Spirit, awakening more of your noble character.

Without having the courage to continually look beyond your physical identity, the splendor of your Soul and the radiance of your Spirit will remain in the Shadow. You can become a beacon of light that brings love and healing into the darkness by simply being yourself, which inevitably allows you to make a contribution to the world you live in. Whether you choose to be an artist, a healer, a banker or a teacher, it is not what you do that counts; it is where you are coming from when you take action. Your individual purpose, or primary focus, is not just about achieving what you want; it is related to the means by which you achieve or the way you succeed – it is about substance.

As you continue to search for deeper meaning and understanding of who you are, and who you are becoming, you can continue to shift your point of perception to encompass more of your True Self. The significance you then place on your experiences will become far more valuable as you develop your ability to garner wisdom. Part of that process is asserting your power as the creator of your own reality and dismantling your Dark Matrix. That level of transformation will enable you to reinstate your spiritual sovereignty and claim your freedom.

The true definition of being spiritual is to have a living, breathing relationship with God/Goddess/All That Is, or the Source, which includes everything in creation. Experiencing life is more important than discovering the meaning of life. You don't live in a vacuum; you have impact. To be aware is to concisely know or recognize the ramifications of your influence. As much as you create your own reality, you also live in a world with other people.

As an individual, you have an effect on the collective unconscious and your thoughts, feelings and actions influence events in the world.

When you raise your level of awareness it subtly impacts everyone like the butterfly effect. This is the phenomenon where a small change that occurs somewhere within a chaotic system, such as the flap of a butterfly's wings, can have large effects on the development of the system, such as the course of the weather a continent away.

If you choose to bypass your Ego, and align with your Authentic Self, you can respond to life with humility and naturally align with the greatest good of all. At which point you shift your awareness from being ego-centric, to world-centric, knowing your impact makes a difference. Your unique spiritual signature is then carried on the wings of grace, conveying a powerful message, which influences the hearts and minds of others. When you reach that point, you can then choose to become cosmo-centric where Soul and Spirit become your priority.

When you fully embrace that concept, you move beyond the 'small story' of your life and align with doing 'The Great Work' – a spiritual transformation that leads to a mystical union with All That Is. The alliance can be seen as harmonious accord between the microcosm (self) and the macrocosm (the universe). Doing The Great Work involves becoming an alchemist and using the force of love to create miracles.

Love is more than an emotion; it is a powerful energy that carries a particular resonance – a frequency you can tap into. The fundamental key to doing The Great Work is genuinely knowing and loving yourself. It is a part of your ultimate destiny – no matter who you are, or where you live. Becoming an alchemist to that degree embellishes your Soul and liberates your Spirit to make a substantial contribution to the world you live in. Your luminous dreams are important. You have the power to make a difference.

You were born with unlimited potential and blessed with a touch of greatness. You have what it takes to strive for and reach that pinnacle point in your Soul's Hologram. There is nothing noble or humble about settling for mediocrity or playing small in the world. Your inherent strengths and talents are your fortune; they are the gifts that allow you to fulfill your True Destiny. Whether of not you use those gifts the choice is yours.

Your courage, commitment and passion can change the course of the collective destiny as well as your own, which is why it is so important to consider your true potential when making choices and decisions. Because the point of power exists in the moment, your choices are pivotal. Wanting others to choose for you relinquishes your authority. Whether it is a partner, a parent, a clairvoyant or a guru, if you place the onus on them to interpret and design your life for you, you will eventually feel incomplete. It will diminish your rapport with your Optimum Future Self.

To stay on course it is imperative you regularly go into peaceful solitude to reflect. Entering the heart of silence, you can sense more of your Soul and the essence of life – the source of love, joy and inspiration. Whether you do that by communing with nature, or taking the time to reflect or meditate, the process is invaluable for lifting your emotions.

The process

Prior to reading this book, you were motivated to know more about your purpose in life and what you are specifically here to do. By this stage of your progress the answers to those questions are within your reach. If you are still haunted by the desire to know more, the following Soul Mapping exercises will provide you with the clarity you need to reach a conclusion. Take into account that having an understanding of your purpose may satisfy your mind but it may not satiate your heart. Remember, experiencing life is more important than discovering the meaning of life. It is the experience of living aligned with your purpose that will bring you the greatest rewards.

During your mapping process, keep in mind that one of your primary lessons is to master the art of conscious creation, while you learn to have fun. You always have the choice of either growing through love and joy or achieving results through struggle and hardship.

To fully understand your primary focus, it is important you define exactly what success is for you. Although success means having access to resources, it is not just about the trappings. To be genuinely successful, your image has to be based on more than wearing the right clothes or having the right car, the right job, or living in a particular neighborhood. You must breathe life into your success or bring aliveness to your creation. Aliveness relates to the depth and quality of your experience and encompasses love, trust, enthusiasm and excited anticipation. It is through loving yourself and sharing your love with others that you become more alive. Being authentic is the key, while you embrace the full range of your emotions. This will allow you to enjoy living a spirited, Soulful life.

There are a few important elements to be considered as you reflect on your primary focus. One is discovering your personal power. Your true power comes from your willingness and ability to choose and then act on your choices. It rests on thinking and feeling and consciously responding to those thoughts and emotions, knowing you have what it takes to succeed. During that process it is important you explore the depth of your creativity and productivity.

Your creativity and productivity are not solely defined by a career or artistic merit. Those labels can be limiting. You are creative when you perceive and conceive. Your level of productivity can be measured by the amount you learn about yourself no matter what you are doing. If you run through a long to-do list and learn little or nothing from your Soul's perspective it can be nonproductive. Productivity is a quality which is based on your ability to produce. It is not a quantity.

Your aim during the exercises will be to identify a clear path that enables you to alter your field of resonance and lift you out of the mire of the general consensus into a new way of being and living. By experiencing the depth and intensity of your emotions you can strengthen your position and shift with grace and elegance. You are becoming an alchemist, harnessing your energy to transmute and transform your reality.

Resonance causation is a powerful form of alchemy that allows you to discover the treasures of your True Self. It is your destiny to have impact on the world and make a difference. It is your feelings that not only make that real; they bring magic and substance to your experience.

Charting your course

Write your intention in your journal. Because you will be working specifically with aligning with your Soul's purpose, use a declaration that aligns with augmenting your strengths and talents.

Perhaps it is something like:

> **'During this level of the course I intend to presence my Soul as often as possible, lifting me into the light and closer to love.'**

Or you may prefer something more direct like:

> **'As I progress through this level of the course I intend to claim the lost depths of my Soul and Spirit.'**

Or

> **'I intend to steer my attention towards the pinnacle point of greatness in my Soul's Hologram and align with oneness.'**

Choose statements that you are genuinely willing to abide by. Make your declaration of intent in the presence of your Higher Self and Soul, so you know you will make every effort to stand by your word.

*Write this **Pocket Affirmation** in your journal and post it in a prominent position to refer to as your daily mantra.*

'I am a beacon of light and a conduit of love, standing on a platform of love, joy individuality and freedom.'

Write the Key Words **Enlightenment versus Illusion** in your journal and contemplate them on a daily basis. Become conscious of which of the two you align with more often, to help you assess where you give your power away.

Do the meditation for this level for a minimum of 15 minutes for at least a week to shift your resonance and move towards love, joy, individuality and freedom. You may want to record any insights in your journal.

Write your answers to the following exercises in your journal.

EXERCISE 30:
Aligning with Greatness

The following exercise will help you to connect with the power and beauty of your Optimum Future Self and the pinnacle point in your Soul's Hologram. As you answer each question, expand your thoughts and allow ideas and images to come to you. Be creative and use your imagination. Don't restrict yourself. Even if you don't have the skills or the means right now your aim is to align with greatness.

Sit quietly and connect with the resonance of your Optimum Future Self and consider your luminous dreams. Imagine you are an ambassador for your Soul.

If you were to deliver one message to the world what would it be? (e.g. peace, joy, love, laughter, compassion, beauty, creativity etc)

What area of the world would you choose to ultimately make a contribution in? (e.g. working with children, animals, ecology, commerce, science, etc)

What strengths has your Future Self developed that you haven't yet?

KEY COORDINATE NO. 18

In your journal, respond to the following in the separate section: Map of the Soul

In a short, succinct sentence, what was your message to the world?

What specific area was your Optimum Future Self working in?

EXERCISE 31 – PART 1:

Charting The Map of the Soul

Drawing up your personal Map of your Soul will give you a visual reference of where you get stopped or give up on your dreams. By looking closely at where your Key Coordinates sit, you can then pinpoint precisely where you need to shift your focus to connect to your Optimum Future Self.

Your aim in the following exercise is to position your Key Coordinates in a way that you can clearly define the Dark and Light Matrix in your Soul's Hologram. This will allow you to see a clear path that leads to the pinnacle point, which aligns with love, joy, individuality and freedom.

The Map of the Soul is illustrated in three tiers:

THE LIGHT MATRIX – What you are here to achieve.

THE TRANSITIONAL THREADS – What you are here to claim as your truth.

THE DARK MATRIX – What you are here to transcend.

Summarize your responses for each of the 18 Key Coordinates you logged over the past 12 levels.

Place each response in the appropriate key coordinate box on your map (see example).

Once you have completed your personal map, take a quiet moment to reflect on the journey of your Soul before you move on to part two of the exercise.

The key coordinates

Light Matrix

Key Coordinate No. 18
PINNACLE POINT

Key Coordinate No. 17   **Key Coordinate No. 16**
FUTURE SELF   LUMINOUS DREAM

Key Coordinate No. 15 **Key Coordinate No. 14** **Key Coordinate No. 13**
ACHIEVEMENTS   STRENGTHS/TALENTS   PRIMARY LESSON

Transitional Threads

Key Coordinate No. 12 **Key Coordinate No. 11** **Key Coordinate No. 10**
NOBLE TRUTH   LIGHT SHADOW   EXPANSIVE STATE

Key Coordinate No. 5   **Key Coordinate No. 4**   **Key Coordinate No. 7**
NEW SCRIPT   POSITIVE IMAGE   NEW LINCHPIN BELIEF

Dark Matrix

Key Coordinate No. 8   **Key Coordinate No. 9**   **Key Coordinate No. 3**
CONTRACTIVE STATE   EMOTIONAL TRIGGER   OLD SCRIPT

Key Coordinate 2   **Key Coordinate No. 6**   **Key Coordinate No. 1**
NEGATIVE IMAGE   OLD LINCHPIN BELIEF   FOCUS

Example

Light Matrix

PINNACLE POINT
Celebrate love and creativity!
Working with children.

FUTURE SELF   **LUMINOUS DREAM**
Gentle, loving and powerful Opening artists co-ops.

ACHIEVEMENTS   **STRENGTHS/TALENTS**   **PRIMARY LESSON**
Exhibiting my work globally   *Artistic, creative,*   *Knowing my worth*
Married to a loving partner   *resourceful,*
Having a family   *determined,*
perceptive, wise

Transitional Threads

NOBLE TRUTH   **LIGHT SHADOW**   **EXPANSIVE STATE**
Nobility   *Desirable/sensual/nurturing*   *Happiness/Passion*

NEW SCRIPT   **POSITIVE IMAGE**   **NEW LINCHPIN BELIEF**
In a intimate relationship   *Cherished*   *I am loved and valued*

Dark Matrix

CONTRACTIVE STATE   **EMOTIONAL TRIGGER**   **OLD SCRIPT**
Loneliness/   *Disappointment/*   *Alone, sad and rejected*
Worthlessness   *Pessimism*

NEGATIVE IMAGE   **OLD LINCHPIN BELIEF**
Outsider   *I will always be alone.*

FOCUS
Love

Navigating Your Way from the Dark to Light Matrix.

This next exercise will help you to alter your resonance and move through the Key Coordinates and transcend your Dark Matrix. Use the ten-step process below to help steer you toward True North, your optimal futures and the Pinnacle Point in your Soul's Hologram. Your aim is to learn how to move from the constrictive emotional frequency of the lowest tier into the transitional threads and then into the Light Matrix.

You can jump from one thread to the next through the power of intention and attention. By using your will, imagination and your capacity to feel, you can completely alter your experience and connect with an alternate future.

Once you are familiar with the process of 'jumping threads', you can use the same ten-step process during your day-to-day life to overcome adversity or augment your success. When you have completed the course, keep your Map of the Soul and the steps on hand so you can easily refer to them whenever you need to shift your thoughts and emotions.

The Ten-Step Process:

1. Identify your position in the lowest tier by getting in touch with your constrictive feelings. Realize they were generated by your trigger emotion, self-image and linchpin belief. This thread or stream of consciousness is the current pattern.
2. Ask yourself if you are genuinely willing to have what you want. Unless your answer is congruently 'yes' you will remain closed and caught in the Dark Matrix.
3. Open up to being receptive and give up your control and resistance. Be humble enough to know things can be different and silence your Objector/Protector. Surrender anything that stands in the way of you having what you want. Whether it is self-pity, martyrdom, victimhood or your resistance to being loved, be willing to let it go and keep giving it up. Realize you are punishing yourself!

4. Move into a state of innocence. Be gentle with yourself to presence your Soul. If you are not sure how to do that, review the meditation from Level 1.

5. Lock in your focus by declaring your intention. Affirm who you are willing to be and what you are willing to have.

6. Shift your resonance to match your Future Self.

7. Practice being grateful in the moment for what you have and what you wish to receive.

8. Take an action, no matter how small, that is consistent with what you ultimately wish to create.

9. Pay attention to who you are becoming and embrace those qualities in the moment. Feel the vibration of the state you wish to be in to amplify and strengthen it.

10. Hold the vision and align with it as much as possible.

EXERCISE 32:

Discovering Your Life's Focus and Ultimate Destiny

Your aim in the following exercise is to review the three tiers of the Map Of The Soul to uncover your Soul's primary focus and discover your True Destiny. This will also help you to clarify your true purpose. Sit quietly and consider the following questions and important elements as you come to a conclusion.

Elements:

Look at your primary life's lesson

Look at your noble truth

Consider your Soul's message to the world.

Questions:

What are you here to transcend?

What are you here to claim as your truth?

What are you here to achieve?

Conclusion:

Write an overview of your Soul's True Purpose and what you ultimately wish to achieve. Keep a copy of your synopsis and make that your primary focus as you approach your future.

MEDITATION

Find a comfortable position and begin to relax. Gently close your eyes.

Allow yourself to go into a deeper state of relaxation. Let your imagination expand and imagine you are making your way through the beauty of nature to the top of mountain. Engage with all of your senses; bringing the sights, smells, sounds and feelings to life.

Imagine yourself slowly ascending, leaving your past behind you. Let go of your self-doubt and any beliefs, attitudes and feelings that no longer serve you. Ready yourself to receive more. As you move to higher ground, feel lighter and freer with every step you take. When you reach the top, sit quietly and look out at the clear vista before you.

Imagine yourself surrounded by a soft, golden light. Take the color in through your breath and allow it to glow brightly in the center of your heart. Acknowledge your essence as a source of love and imagine that there are tiny threads of golden light connecting you to the heart and essence of All That Is. Feel your heart opening and allow yourself to be in harmony with everything in creation. Rest in the tranquility and sense the grace that permeates your being.

Visualize a source of silver light above your head. Let your consciousness expand as you attune to the universal mind.

Feel yourself being energized as you visualize your radiant Future Self. Imagine yourself as a successful, confident being, with a strong sense of courage and achievement. Let your imagination come alive, while enjoying the magnificence of your dreams and aspirations gracefully unfolding before you.

Intensify your feelings and bask in the resonance of success. Take a moment to declare what you wish to achieve and what you are willing to receive. Bring your attention back to your body, take a deep breath and gently bring yourself out of the meditation.

Your checklist

1. Did you write in your journal on a regular basis to observe your thoughts and feelings?
2. Did you record any Soul-Speak?
3. Have you logged your insights, goals and aspirations?
4. Were you mindful of your intention?
5. Did you take time to contemplate the Divine Truth and the two Key Words?
6. Have you been using your Pocket Affirmation on a regular basis?
7. Have you taken the time to meditate for a minimum of 15 minutes on at least three occasions?
8. Have you done your exercises and logged them?
9. Have you been focusing on your True Purpose and Ultimate Destiny to support your Heart's Desire?
10. If you haven't done any or all of these things then ask yourself – what stopped you?

You may be going into denial or avoidance around the topic for this particular level of self-discovery – what has your Ego been telling you? Those conversations reflect your limited beliefs about yourself. CHALLENGE THEM! Remember – your heart's desires are at stake.

Conclusion

Staying On Course

Now that you have completed the course, your challenge will be to keep up your momentum. The principles and theories you have learnt during the past few months can become more than just concepts; they can become your truth. Those principles illustrate how creating your reality works. The awareness you have gained has broadened your understanding and can be integrated into wisdom. That means living as a spiritual person who practices metaphysics 24 hours a day and not just on certain occasions.

Using the techniques consistently will liberate you. You can then become the alchemist, visionary and co-creator that you are destined to be. There is always more to create; you are living within a reality of expanding dreams.

To stay on course, listen and respond to your Soul's whispers; they will always guide you home to your heart and set you on the path of True North. If you approach life with a 'beginner's mind' in that state of innocence, you can look at the world each day with wonder and awe as if you are seeing it for the very first time. In that receptive state, you are far more likely to perceive the goodness, truth and beauty that is always present. Maintaining that view will allow you to experience a new way of being and a new way of living.

To quote Einstein,

'The significant problems we face cannot be solved at the same level of thinking we were at when we created them.'

Which is why it is so important that you continue to expand your way of thinking.

He also said,

'Imagination is more important than knowledge. Knowledge is limited. Imagination encircles the world.'

From a metaphysical standpoint, you conceive life through your imagination first – not through logic. It is up to you to 'dream the dream' and bring that reality into creation by remaining humble and continuously shifting your focus.

The path to higher consciousness is only possible when you bypass your Ego to honor the power and beauty of your Soul and Spirit. It pays to continually monitor which part of you is steering your course. You always have the choice of either yielding to love or upholding control. Your biggest challenge will be confronting the Objector/Protector, who robs you of your happiness. Whether it appears as the dream stealer, saboteur or critical parent, it must be rendered powerless.

When you find keeping to this truth difficult, or if you hit a wall or fall into an emotional pothole, run through the suggestions below and find one that works for you. Remember – your point of power is in the moment and your power comes from your ability to take action.

10 Tips to Keep You On Track –

1. Meditate and journal every day to help you stay mindful.
2. Challenge the Objector/Protector and disengage from your Ego as often as possible throughout your day.
3. Give up anything that stands in the way of you having what you want on a regular basis. Whether this obstacle is an addiction, self-pity, control, martyrdom or your resistance to being loved, be willing to let it go and keep giving it up. Your choice here is self-love or self-punishment!
4. Be humble and stay receptive. Move into a state of innocence as often as possible.
5. If your emotions are heavy and keeping you stuck – do something to move your energy! You may want to meditate, write in your journal, go for a walk in nature, listen to your favorite music, have a bath or shower, have a massage, read some uplifting material or call an inspiring friend. Whatever it takes, shift your state!
6. Read the Divine Truth outlined below on a daily basis. Make it your creed.
7. Be the Objective Observer – don't react and get hooked – detach and shift your perception.
8. Remind yourself that you are living in a dream. The physical world is an illusion - it is not real!
9. Be true to yourself. Align with your Authentic Self as often as possible.
10. Love your Soul and Spirit – they are worthy of being honored and cherished.

The divine truth

1. Your point of power exists in the moment.
2. You were born with the power to create your own reality and determine the course of your destiny. You either consciously create your reality, or subconsciously allow events to take place in your world.
3. What you create in your physical world is a reflection of your own beliefs.
4. To experience love and freedom, you have to be willing to give up control.
5. You have free will.
6. You are whole and complete – there is nothing missing inside of you.
7. You live in a world filled with love, abundance and joy. The way you perceive your world determines your experience.
8. What you receive is based on what you are willing to have and not on what you deserve.
9. Life is a gift from God/Goddess/All That Is and you are here to learn to receive.
10. The physical world is an illusion – so you can have as much of the illusion as you like.
11. You are a part of the process of evolution – you are who you are becoming and not just who you have been.
12. You can be anyone, have anything and do anything you choose, with harm to none.